RICE & RISOTTO

THE AUSTRALIAN
Women's Weekly

contents

One of the most versatile ingredients to keep in your pantry, this humble grain segues between cuisines and courses with such ease, it is sure to become your new best friend in the kitchen. We've developed a bundle of fantastic rice recipes for you to try; from Italian risotto to Turkish pilaf, sushi rice to a traditional baked rice custard, we've certainly covered all bases. Inexpensive, easy to cook and even easier to eat, there's no reason not to love rice.

Pamela Clark
Food Director

spicy chicken fried rice

preparation time 15 minutes cooking time 30 minutes serves 4

2 teaspoons peanut oil

2 eggs, beaten lightly

500g chicken thigh fillets, sliced thinly

2 medium brown onions (300g), chopped finely

1 tablespoon ground cumin

2 teaspoons ground coriander

¼ teaspoon cardamom seeds

1 teaspoon ground cinnamon

2 fresh small red thai chillies, seeded, chopped finely

2 cloves garlic, crushed

1 large red capsicum (350g), sliced thinly

115g fresh baby corn, halved lengthways

500g packet frozen pre-cooked rice

4 green onions, sliced finely

2 tablespoons ketjap manis

2 tablespoons coarsely chopped fresh coriander

1 Heat ½ teaspoon of the oil in wok or large pan, add half the egg, swirl so egg forms a thin omelette; cook until set.

2 Transfer omelette to board, roll, cut into thin strips. Repeat with remaining egg and another ½ teaspoon oil. Heat remaining oil in wok; stir-fry chicken and brown onion, in batches, until chicken is tender. Stir-fry spices, chilli and garlic in wok until fragrant. Add capsicum and corn; stir-fry until just tender. Return chicken mixture to wok with omelette strips, rice, green onion, ketjap manis and coriander; stir-fry until hot.

PER SERVING *11.9g fat; 1887kJ (451 cal)*

RICE

khitcherie

preparation time 25 minutes (plus standing time) cooking time 30 minutes serves 4

1 cup (200g) toor dhal (yellow split peas)

¼ cup ghee

1 medium brown onion (150g), chopped finely

2 cloves garlic, crushed

2 small green chillies, chopped finely

2 teaspoons finely grated fresh ginger

½ teaspoon ground turmeric

1 teaspoon cumin seeds

½ teaspoon garam masala

1 teaspoon ground coriander

1 cinnamon stick

4 curry leaves

2 teaspoons salt

1½ cups (300g) basmati rice, washed, drained

1 cup (170g) raisins

4 cups (1 litre) hot water

1 tablespoon lime juice

½ cup (75g) cashews, toasted

1 Place dhal in small bowl, cover with cold water; soak 1 hour. Drain well.

2 Heat ghee in medium saucepan; cook brown onion, garlic, chilli, ginger, spices, curry leaves and salt, stirring, until onion is browned lightly and mixture is fragrant.

3 Add dhal, rice, raisins and water; boil, then immediately simmer, covered, 15 minutes or until rice is tender. Remove from heat, discard cinnamon, stir in juice; stand, covered, 5 minutes. Just before serving, stir in cashews.
   PER SERVING *24.1g fat; 3336kJ (798 cal)*

aromatic rice

1 tablespoon ghee

2 small brown onions (160g), sliced finely

3 cloves garlic, crushed

3 teaspoons cumin seeds

2 teaspoons black mustard seeds

4 cardamom pods, bruised

2 bay leaves

½ cup (75g) shelled pistachio nuts

1½ cups (300g) basmati rice, washed, drained

2¾ cups (680ml) warm chicken stock

1 Heat ghee in medium heavy-based saucepan; cook onions, garlic, spices and nuts, stirring, 5 minutes or until onions are browned lightly and mixture is fragrant.

2 Stir in rice and warm stock; simmer, covered, 15 minutes. Remove from heat; fluff with fork, then stand, covered, 10 minutes.

PER SERVING *5g fat; 610kJ (146 cal)*

lemon and saffron rice

4 cups (1 litre) chicken stock

¼ teaspoon saffron threads

2 tablespoons ghee

2 small brown onions (160g), sliced

2 cloves garlic, crushed

1 teaspoon grated fresh ginger

6 curry leaves

2 teaspoons grated lemon rind

2 cups (400g) basmati rice, washed, drained

¼ cup (60ml) lemon juice

¼ cup chopped fresh coriander

1 Bring stock to boil in medium saucepan, remove from heat, stir in saffron; cover, stand 15 minutes.

2 Heat ghee in medium saucepan; cook onion, garlic, ginger and curry leaves, stirring, until onion is browned lightly. Stir in rind and rice.

3 Add stock to rice mixture; simmer, covered, 15 minutes or until rice is tender and liquid absorbed. Stir in juice and fresh coriander; stand, covered, 5 minutes.

PER SERVING *10.3g fat; 1994kJ (477 cal)*

nawabi biryani

preparation time 20 minutes (plus standing time) cooking time 30 minutes serves 4

2 tablespoons ghee

2 medium brown onions (300g), sliced thinly

2 medium potatoes (400g), chopped

1 teaspoon cumin seeds

2 cups (400g) long-grain rice

4 cups (1 litre) water

1 cup (125g) frozen peas

MINT MASALA

½ cup firmly packed fresh mint leaves

2 long green chillies, chopped

2 tablespoons vegetable oil

½ teaspoon garam masala

1 teaspoon salt

¼ cup (35g) coconut milk powder

¼ cup (60ml) water

1 Heat ghee in large saucepan; cook onion and potato, stirring, until both are just browned lightly.

2 Make mint masala.

3 Add cumin seeds and mint masala to pan; cook, stirring, until fragrant. Stir in rice.

4 Add water to pan; simmer, covered, 10 minutes. Remove from heat, stir in peas; stand, covered, 10 minutes.

MINT MASALA Blend or process all ingredients until pureed.

PER SERVING *21.1g fat; 2813kJ (673 cal)*

caramelised onion, fruit and nut pilau

preparation time 15minutes (plus standing time) cooking time 35 minutes serves 4

2 tablespoons ghee

2 large brown onions (400g), sliced

2 tablespoons ghee, extra

1 teaspoon hot chilli powder

1 teaspoon ground black pepper

¼ teaspoon saffron threads

4 cardamom pods, bruised

4 cloves

1 cinnamon stick

1 teaspoon salt

2 cups (400g) basmati rice, washed, drained

4 cups (1 litre) water

½ cup (75g) currants

½ cup (75g) chopped dried apricots

½ cup (80g) sultanas

½ cup (70g) slivered almonds, toasted

1 Heat ghee in large saucepan; cook onion, stirring, 15 minutes or until caramelised. Remove from pan.

2 Add extra ghee and spices to same pan; cook, stirring until fragrant. Stir in salt, rice and onion.

3 Add water; boil, then immediately simmer, covered, 10 minutes or until rice is tender and water absorbed. Stir in currants, apricots and sultanas; stand, covered, 5 minutes. Just before serving, stir in nuts.

PER SERVING *27.9g fat; 3361kJ (804 cal)*

tomato pilau

preparation time 15 minutes (plus standing time) cooking time 30 minutes serves 4

2 cups (400g) basmati rice washed, drained

2 tablespoons ghee

1 large brown onion (200g), chopped

1 cinnamon stick

4 cardamom pods, bruised

4 cloves

½ teaspoon chilli powder

1 teaspoon ground cumin

1 teaspoon ground coriander

1¼ cups (310ml) chicken stock

1 cup (250ml) tomato juice

1 teaspoon salt

2 large tomatoes (500g), chopped

¼ cup chopped fresh coriander

1 cup (80g) flaked almonds, toasted

½ cup (75g) currants

1 Place rice in medium bowl, cover with water; stand 20 minutes. Drain well.

2 Heat ghee in large pan; cook onion, cinnamon, cardamom and cloves, stirring, until onion is browned lightly. Add the ground spices; cook, stirring, until fragrant. Stir in rice.

3 Add stock, juice and salt; boil then immediately simmer, covered, for about 10 minutes, stirring occasionally, or until rice is tender and liquid absorbed. Discard cinnamon stick.

4 Stir in tomatoes, coriander leaves, nuts and currants; stand, covered, for 5 minutes.
   PER SERVING *20.9g fat; 2767kJ (662 cal)*

TIP Best made just before serving.

kedgeree

preparation time 10 minutes cooking time 25 minutes serves 4

You will need approximately 1¼ cups of uncooked long-grain rice for this recipe.

1 tablespoon vegetable oil

1 medium brown onion (150g), chopped finely

1 tablespoon mild curry paste

3 cups cooked long-grain white rice

415g canned salmon, drained, flaked

¼ cup (60ml) cream

2 hard-boiled eggs

2 tablespoons finely chopped fresh flat-leaf parsley

1 Heat oil in large pan; cook onion, stirring, until soft. Add curry paste; cook, stirring, until fragrant. Stir in rice, salmon and cream; cook, stirring, until hot. Just before serving, cut each egg into 6 wedges and gently stir through kedgeree; sprinkle with parsley.
PER SERVING 26.4g fat; 3612kJ (864 cal)

spinach pilau

preparation time 15 minutes cooking time 30 minutes serves 4

2 tablespoons vegetable oil

6 green onions, sliced

2 dried red chillies, crushed

½ teaspoon coriander seeds

1 clove garlic, crushed

2 cups (400g) long-grain rice

4 cups (1 litre) water

1 tablespoon chicken stock powder

500g spinach, chopped

¼ cup chopped fresh basil

½ cup (125ml) yogurt

1 Heat vegetable oil in medium saucepan; cook onion, chilli, seeds and garlic, stirring, until fragrant.

2 Stir in rice; add water and stock powder. Boil; immediately simmer, covered, 15 minutes or until rice is tender and liquid absorbed.

3 Remove from heat; stir in spinach, basil and yogurt.
PER SERVING 11.6g fat; 2077kJ (497 cal)

leek, prosciutto and rice frittata

preparation time 15 minutes (plus standing time) cooking time 45 minutes serves 4

1 tablespoon olive oil

2 medium leeks (700g), chopped

3 slices prosciutto (45g), chopped

7 eggs, lightly beaten

¼ cup (20g) grated parmesan cheese

½ cup (125ml) buttermilk

1 cup cooked white short-grain rice

¼ cup chopped fresh chives

1 Preheat oven to 180°C/160°C fan-forced. Grease deep 19cm square cake pan.

2 Heat oil in frying pan; add leek and prosciutto, cook, stirring, until leek is soft. Combine leek mixture with remaining ingredients in bowl; mix well.

3 Pour mixture into prepared cake pan, bake, uncovered, in oven about 35 minutes or until lightly browned and set. Stand for 5 minutes before turning out.
   PER SERVING *17.2g fat; 1338kJ (320 cal)*

wild rice salad

preparation time 20 minutes cooking time 45 minutes serves 6

1 cup (180g) wild rice

2 cups (400g) brown rice

2 sticks celery, sliced finely

310g canned corn kernels, drained

4 medium tomatoes (760g), seeded, sliced thinly

⅔ cup (160ml) oil-free French dressing

2 cloves garlic, crushed

⅓ cup finely chopped fresh flat-leaf parsley

1 Cook wild rice in large pan of boiling water, uncovered, until just tender; drain. Rinse under cold water; drain.

2 Meanwhile, cook brown rice in another large pan of boiling water, uncovered, until just tender; drain. Rinse under cold water; drain.

3 Combine wild rice and brown rice in large bowl with celery, corn and tomato. Add combined dressing, garlic and parsley; mix well.
   PER SERVING *2.9g fat; 1700kJ (406 cal)*

soy beans and rice

1¼ cups (250g) dried soy beans

1 tablespoon olive oil

2 cloves garlic, crushed

2 large brown onions (400g), chopped finely

2 tablespoons grated lemon rind

1¼ cups (250g) long-grain white rice, rinsed, drained

2½ cups (625ml) chi cken stock

50g butter

1 teaspoon ground cinnamon

1⅓ cups (200g) dried apricots

1¼ cups (210g) seeded prunes, halved

⅓ cup (80ml) lemon juice

1 Place beans in large bowl, cover with cold water; soak overnight.

2 Rinse and drain beans, add beans to large pan of boiling water; simmer, uncovered, about 1 hour or until beans are tender. Drain.

3 Heat oil in same pan; cook garlic, onion and rind, stirring, until onion is soft. Add beans, rice and stock, bring to boil; simmer, covered, about 20 minutes or until rice is just tender. (Can be made ahead to this stage. Cover; refrigerate overnight.)

4 Meanwhile, melt butter in medium pan; cook cinnamon, apricots, prunes and juice, stirring, until apricots are browned lightly. Serve beans and rice topped with dried fruit, drizzled with pan juices.
PER SERVING *28.8g fat; 3390kJ (811 cal)*

easy fried rice

preparation time 25 minutes cooking time 25 minutes serves 4

2 teaspoons peanut oil

2 eggs, beaten lightly

1 teaspoon sesame oil

4 bacon rashers (280g), chopped coarsely

1 medium brown onion (150g), chopped coarsely

2 trimmed sticks celery (150g), sliced thickly

1 clove garlic, crushed

1 tablespoon grated fresh ginger

3 cups cold cooked long-grain white rice

100g cooked shelled small prawns

425g canned baby corn, drained, sliced thinly

½ cup (125g) frozen peas, thawed

4 green onions, sliced thinly

1 tablespoon soy sauce

1 Heat 1 teaspoon of the peanut oil in heated large wok or heavy-base frying pan. Cook half of the egg; swirl wok to make a thin omelette. Remove omelette from wok; roll omelette and cut into thin strips. Repeat with remaining egg.

2 Heat remaining peanut oil and sesame oil in wok; stir-fry bacon until brown. Add brown onion, celery, garlic and ginger; stir-fry over high heat until vegetables are just tender.

3 Add rice, omelette and remaining ingredients to wok; stir-fry, tossing, until well combined and heated through.
PER SERVING *10.8g fat; 1586kJ (379 cal)*

TIP Fried rice is best made just before serving.

coconut pilaf

preparation time 10 minutes cooking time 35 minutes serves 4

¼ cup ghee

2 medium brown onions (300g), sliced thinly

1 teaspoon cumin seeds

1 cinnamon stick

4 cardamom pods, bruised

3 whole cloves

1 teaspoon turmeric

1 cup (200g) basmati rice

1⅔ cups (410ml) coconut cream

½ cup (125ml) water

½ cup (75g) pistachios, toasted, chopped coarsely

¼ cup (35g) currants

1 Melt ghee in large frying pan; cook onion, stirring over medium heat about 4 minutes or until soft. Stir in seeds, cinnamon, cardamom, cloves and turmeric; stir over medium heat 2 minutes.

2 Stir in rice; stir over heat a further minute. Stir in coconut cream and the water; bring to a boil. Reduce heat; simmer, covered, about 20 minutes or until all liquid is absorbed and rice is tender. Remove and discard cinnamon stick. Stir through nuts and currants. Stir pilaf with fork before serving.
PER SERVING *45.3g fat; 2757kJ (659 cal)*

barley risotto with chicken and tarragon

preparation time 15 minutes **cooking time** 40 minutes **serves** 4

Pearl barley is barley that has had the husk removed, then been hulled and polished, much the same as rice.

1 tablespoon olive oil

500g chicken breast fillets, sliced thinly

3 cups (750ml) chicken stock

2 cups (500ml) water

1 medium brown onion (150g), chopped finely

1 clove garlic, crushed

2 medium leeks (700g), sliced thinly

¾ cup (150g) pearl barley

⅓ cup (80ml) dry white wine

1 cup (120g) frozen peas

2 tablespoons finely shredded fresh tarragon

1   Heat half of the oil in large saucepan; cook chicken, in batches, until browned lightly and cooked through. Cover to keep warm.

2   Meanwhile, combine stock and the water in large saucepan; bring to a boil. Reduce heat; simmer, covered.

3   Meanwhile, heat remaining oil in cleaned pan; cook onion, garlic and leek, stirring, until onion softens. Add barley; stir to combine with onion mixture. Add wine; cook, stirring, until almost evaporated. Stir in ½ cup of the simmering stock mixture; cook, stirring, over low heat until liquid is absorbed. Continue adding stock mixture, in ½-cup batches, stirring until absorbed after each addition. Total cooking time should be about 30 minutes or until barley is just tender.

4   Add chicken and peas to risotto; cook, stirring, until peas are just tender. Remove from heat; stir in tarragon.
PER SERVING *9 .7g fat; 1584kJ (379 cal)*

RISOTTO

lemon risotto

preparation time 15 minutes cooking time 40 minutes serves 4

4 cups (1 litre) chicken stock

1 cup (250ml) dry white wine

2 teaspoons finely grated lemon rind

1 tablespoon lemon juice

80g butter

1 medium brown onion (150g), chopped finely

2 cups (400g) arborio rice

¾ cup (60g) finely grated parmesan cheese

2 tablespoons finely chopped fresh flat-leaf parsley

1   Bring stock and wine to boil in medium saucepan, add rind and juice; simmer, covered, while preparing onion and rice.

2   Heat half of the butter in large saucepan; cook onion, stirring, until soft. Add rice; stir over medium heat until coated in butter mixture and slightly changed in colour.

3   Uncover stock mixture; add 1 cup to rice mixture. Cook, stirring, over medium heat until liquid is absorbed.

4   Continue adding stock mixture, 1 cup at a time, stirring constantly, until liquid is absorbed between additions. Total cooking time should be about 35 minutes or until rice is just tender.

5   Remove pan from heat; stir in remaining butter, cheese and parsley. Serve immediately.

PER SERVING *22.1g fat; 2805kJ (670 cal)*

TIP You can use olive oil rather than butter, or equal amounts of each.

risotto milanese

preparation time 15 minutes cooking time 40 minutes serves 6

90g butter

1 large brown onion (200g), chopped finely

375g arborio rice

½ cup (125ml) dry white wine

3 cups (750ml) hot chicken stock

¼ teaspoon saffron powder

2 tablespoons grated parmesan cheese

1 Heat two-thirds (60g) of the butter in large saucepan; cook onion until tender, stirring gently.

2 Add rice to pan; stir until well coated with butter mixture.

3 Add wine, 1 cup (250ml) of the stock and saffron to pan; stir. Bring to a boil; when liquid is almost evaporated, add another 1 cup (250ml) of the stock. Stir; bring to a boil. When liquid is almost evaporated, stir in remaining stock; reduce heat. Cook until stock is absorbed. (Cooking time is about 30 minutes from the time the first cup of stock is added. Cook rice uncovered during this time.)

4 Stir in remaining butter and cheese; stir gently until butter melts.
   PER SERVING *13.7g fat; 1544kJ (369 cal)*

artichoke risotto

preparation time 10 minutes cooking time 25 minutes serves 6

2 teaspoons olive oil

1 medium brown onion (150g), chopped finely

3 cloves garlic, crushed

6 green onions, sliced thinly

2 cups (400g) arborio rice

¾ cup (180ml) dry white wine

1½ cups (375ml) chicken stock

3 cups (750ml) water

400g can artichoke hearts, drained, sliced thinly

½ cup (40g) finely grated parmesan cheese

1 Heat oil in large saucepan; cook brown onion, garlic and half of the green onion, stirring, until brown onion softens. Add rice, wine, stock and the water; bring to a boil. Reduce heat; simmer, covered, 15 minutes, stirring occasionally.

2 Stir in artichoke, cheese and remaining green onion; cook, stirring, about 5 minutes or until artichokes are heated through.
   PER SERVING *4.5g fat; 1353kJ (323 cal)*

TIP A salad of grape tomatoes, sliced fennel and a few fresh basil leaves suits this risotto perfectly.

mushroom and spinach risotto

preparation time 10 minutes cooking time 25 minutes serves 4

10g butter

1 medium brown onion (150g), chopped coarsely

1 clove garlic, crushed

2 cups (400g) arborio rice

1 cup (250ml) dry white wine

2 cups (500ml) vegetable stock

1½ cups (375ml) water

150g button mushrooms, sliced thickly

1 bunch spinach (500g), trimmed,
chopped coarsely

¼ cup loosely packed, coarsely chopped
fresh flat-leaf parsley

¾ cup (60g) coarsely grated parmesan cheese

1 Place butter, onion and garlic in a large microwave-safe dish; cook on HIGH (100%) 2 minutes or until onion softens. Add rice, stir; cook, covered, on HIGH (100%) 1 minute. Add wine, stock and the water, stir; cook, covered, on HIGH (100%) 15 minutes, stirring occasionally.

2 Add mushrooms, stir; cook, covered, on HIGH (100%) 5 minutes, or until most of the liquid is absorbed.

3 Transfer risotto to a large serving bowl; stir through spinach, parsley and parmesan cheese.
   PER SERVING 8.3g fat; 2193kJ (524 cal)

shellfish paella risotto

preparation time 30 minutes cooking time 45 minutes serves 4

24 uncooked medium prawns (600g)

16 large black mussels (500g)

200g salmon fillet

3 cups (750ml) chicken stock

3 cups (750ml) water

½ cup (125ml) dry white wine

4 saffron threads, toasted, crushed

1 large red capsicum (350g)

2 large tomatoes (500g)

1 cup (125g) frozen peas

1 tablespoon olive oil

1 large brown onion (200g), chopped finely

2 cloves garlic, crushed

1½ cups (300g) arborio rice

1   Shell and devein prawns, leaving tails intact. Scrub mussels; remove beards. Heat small oiled frying pan; cook salmon until browned both sides and just cooked through.

2   Combine stock, the water, wine and saffron in large saucepan; bring to a boil. Reduce heat; simmer, covered, over low heat.

3   Meanwhile, cut capsicum in half lengthways. Discard seeds and membranes; chop capsicum finely. Peel tomatoes; seed and chop finely. Rinse peas under hot water; drain.

4   Heat oil in large saucepan; cook onion, garlic and capsicum, stirring, until onion softens. Add rice; stir to coat in onion mixture. Stir in 1-cup batches of the hot stock mixture; cook, stirring, until liquid is absorbed after each addition. Total cooking time should be about 35 minutes or until rice is just tender and all the liquid has been absorbed.

5   Add prawns and mussels; cook, stirring, until prawns change in colour and mussels open. Discard any mussels that do not open. Add tomato, peas and flaked salmon; stir gently until risotto is heated through.
PER SERVING *10.5g fat; 2260kJ (540 cal)*

TIP Saffron threads should be toasted in a small dry frying pan over medium heat until they are just fragrant, then crushed with the back of a spoon (or crumbled with your fingers directly over the saucepan).

vegetable risotto

preparation time 10 minutes (plus standing time) cooking time 45 minutes serves 2

1 small eggplant (230g), chopped finely

salt

2 teaspoons olive oil

1 small brown onion (80g), chopped finely

1 clove garlic, crushed

¾ cup (150g) brown rice

¾ cup (80ml) chicken stock

2 cups (500ml) water

2 medium zucchini (240g)

2 medium tomatoes (380g), peeled, chopped finely

125g mushrooms, sliced thinly

¼ cup (20g) coarsely grated parmesan cheese

1 tablespoon fresh oregano leaves

1 Place eggplant in colander; sprinkle with salt. Stand for 30 minutes; rinse well under cold water. Pat dry with absorbent paper.

2 Heat oil in large saucepan; cook onion and garlic until soft. Add rice, stock and the water; bring to boil. Simmer, covered, for about 30 minutes or until rice is tender and almost all the liquid is absorbed.

3 Using a vegetable peeler, cut zucchini into ribbons.

4 Stir eggplant, zucchini, tomato and mushroom into rice; cook for about 3 minutes or until vegetables are softened. Stir in half the cheese and oregano; serve risotto sprinkled with remaining cheese.
PER SERVING 11.2g fat; 1923kJ (460 cal)

TIP Risotto best made just before serving.

roasted vegetable risotto

preparation time 15 minutes cooking time 45 minutes serves 4

1 large red capsicum (350g), sliced thickly

2 small finger eggplants (120g), sliced thinly

2 small zucchini (120g), sliced thinly

1 medium red onion (150g), cut into wedges

¼ cup (60ml) olive oil

5 cups (1.25 litres) chicken stock

1 cup (250ml) white wine

50g butter

1 medium brown onion (150g), chopped finely

2½ cups (500g) arborio rice

½ cup (80g) finely grated parmesan cheese

2 tablespoons finely shredded fresh basil

1 Place capsicum, eggplant, zucchini and red onion in large baking dish; coat with oil. Roast in hot oven about 30 minutes or until tender.

2 Meanwhile, combine stock and wine in medium saucepan; bring to a boil. Reduce heat; simmer.

3 Melt butter in large saucepan; cook brown onion, stirring, until soft. Add rice; stir to coat in butter. Add about 1 cup of the simmering stock mixture; cook, stirring, over low heat until liquid is absorbed between each addition.

4 Stir through cheese and basil. Serve with roasted vegetables.
PER SERVING 32.7g fat; 3617kJ (864 cal)

mixed mushroom risotto

preparation time 10 minutes cooking time 45 minutes serves 4

3 cups (750ml) chicken stock

2 cups (500ml) water

1 tablespoon olive oil

200g swiss brown mushrooms, quartered

150g oyster mushrooms, halved

200g button mushrooms, halved

2 cloves garlic, crushed

1 medium brown onion (150g), chopped coarsely

2 cups (400g) arborio rice

1 tablespoon finely chopped fresh tarragon

⅓ cup (80g) sour cream

1 tablespoon wholegrain mustard

1 Bring stock and the water to a boil in large saucepan. Reduce heat; simmer, uncovered, while cooking mushrooms.

2 Heat half of the oil in large saucepan; cook mushrooms, in batches, until just tender.

3 Heat remaining oil in same pan; cook garlic and onion, stirring, until onion softens. Add rice to pan; stir over medium heat until slightly changed in colour. Stir in 1-cup batches of the hot stock mixture; cook, over medium heat, stirring, until liquid is absorbed after each addition.

4 Add mushrooms and tarragon to risotto when last cup of stock mixture has been added and is almost absorbed. Total cooking time for rice should be about 35 minutes or until rice is just tender. Serve risotto topped with combined sour cream and mustard.

PER SERVING *14.3g fat; 2234kJ (534 cal)*

broad bean risotto with crispy bacon, parmesan and sage

preparation time 10 minutes cooking time 45 minutes serves 4

6 cups (1.5 litres) chicken stock

½ cup (125ml) dry white wine

2 tablespoons olive oil

4 green onions, chopped finely

2 cloves garlic, crushed

2 cups (400g) arborio rice

6 bacon rashers (420g), halved

½ cup (125ml) cream

1 cup (80g) finely grated parmesan cheese

500g packet frozen broad beans, cooked, peeled

1 tablespoon coarsely chopped fresh sage

½ cup (40g) parmesan cheese flakes

1 Bring stock and wine to a boil in medium saucepan; reduce heat. Cover; keep hot.

2 Heat oil in large saucepan; cook onion and garlic, stirring, until onion is soft. Add rice; stir to coat in oil mixture. Stir in 1 cup of the hot stock mixture; cook over low heat, stirring, until liquid is absorbed.

3 Continue adding stock mixture, in 1-cup batches, stirring until absorbed after each addition. Total cooking time should be about 35 minutes or until rice is just tender.

4 Meanwhile, cook bacon under heated grill until browned and crisp on both sides.

5 Remove risotto from heat; stir in cream, grated cheese, beans and sage. Serve topped with bacon and flaked cheese.
PER SERVING *56.1g fat; 4469kJ (1068 cal)*

TIP You can replace the broad beans with frozen peas, if preferred.

beetroot risotto with rocket

preparation time 20 minutes cooking time 45 minutes serves 4

2 medium beetroot (350g), peeled, grated coarsely

3 cups (750ml) vegetable stock

3 cups (750ml) water

1 tablespoon olive oil

1 large brown onion (200g), chopped finely

2 cloves garlic, crushed

1½ cups (300g) arborio rice

¼ cup (20g) coarsely grated parmesan cheese

50g baby rocket leaves

1 tablespoon finely chopped fresh flat-leaf parsley

1 Combine beetroot, stock and the water in large saucepan; bring to a boil. Reduce heat; simmer, uncovered.

2 Meanwhile, heat oil in large saucepan; cook onion and garlic, stirring, until onion softens. Add rice; stir rice to coat in onion mixture. Stir in 1 cup simmering beetroot mixture; cook, stirring, over low heat until liquid is absorbed. Continue adding beetroot mixture, in 1-cup batches, stirring, until liquid is absorbed after each addition. Total cooking time should be about 35 minutes or until rice is just tender; gently stir in cheese.

3 Serve beetroot risotto topped with combined rocket and parsley.
   PER SERVING *7.6g fat; 1643kJ (393 cal)*

risotto primavera

preparation time 10 minutes cooking time 25 minutes serves 4

Primavera is the Italian word for spring and the season's freshest produce is used in this risotto, which is produced by a labour-saving covered cooking method.

20g butter

2 teaspoons olive oil

1 medium leek (350g), sliced thinly

1 clove garlic, crushed

2 cups (400g) arborio rice

¾ cup (180ml) dry white wine

1½ cups (375ml) vegetable stock

2½ cups (625ml) water

150g sugar snap peas

300g asparagus, sliced thickly

100g yellow patty-pan squash, quartered

⅔ cup (50g) finely grated parmesan cheese

⅓ cup (80ml) cream

1 Heat butter and oil in large saucepan; cook leek and garlic, stirring, until leek softens.

2 Add rice, wine, stock and the water, bring to a boil; reduce heat, simmer, covered, 15 minutes, stirring occasionally.

3 Stir in peas, asparagus and squash; cook, covered, about 5 minutes or until rice is just tender.

4 Just before serving, stir in cheese and cream.
   PER SERVING *20.4g fat; 2632kJ (629 cal)*

risotto-filled zucchini flowers

preparation time 50 minutes cooking time 50 minutes makes 48

1 cup (250ml) dry white wine

2 cups (500ml) vegetable stock

½ cup (125ml) water

1 tablespoon olive oil

1 small brown onion (80g), chopped finely

1 clove garlic, crushed

1 cup (200g) arborio rice

150g mushrooms, sliced thinly

2 trimmed silver beet leaves (160g), chopped finely

¼ cup (20g) finely grated parmesan cheese

48 tiny zucchini with flowers attached

cooking-oil spray

1 Combine wine, stock and the water in large saucepan; bring to a boil. Reduce heat; simmer, covered, to keep hot.

2 Meanwhile, heat oil in large saucepan; cook onion and garlic, stirring, until onion softens. Add rice; stir to coat in onion mixture. Stir in 1 cup of the hot stock mixture; cook, stirring, over low heat until liquid is absorbed. Continue adding hot stock mixture, in 1-cup batches, stirring, until liquid is absorbed after each addition. Total cooking time should be about 35 minutes or until rice is tender.

3 Add mushrooms and silver beet; cook, stirring, until mushrooms are just tender. Stir in cheese.

4 Remove and discard stamens from centre of flowers; fill flowers with risotto, twist petal tops to enclose filling.

5 Cook zucchini with flowers, in batches, on heated oiled grill plate (or grill or barbecue) until zucchini are just tender and risotto is heated through. Serve hot.

PER FLOWER *0.7g fat; 121kJ (29 cal)*

TIP Risotto can be prepared a day ahead. Spread risotto on tray, cover; refrigerate until required.

onion and fennel risotto with chicken meatballs

preparation time 40 minutes cooking time 3 hours 30 minutes serves 6

12 cups (3 litres) water

1kg chicken bones

1 large carrot (180g), chopped coarsely

1 trimmed celery stalk (100g), chopped coarsely

1 small brown onion (80g), chopped coarsely

1 bay leaf

2 sprigs fresh flat-leaf parsley

1 teaspoon black peppercorns

2 cups (500ml) dry white wine

1 tablespoon olive oil

20g butter

2 medium brown onions (300g), sliced thinly

1 large fennel (550g), trimmed, sliced thinly

3 cups (600g) arborio rice

2 cloves garlic, crushed

1 cup (80g) coarsely grated parmesan cheese

2 tablespoons finely chopped fresh tarragon

CHICKEN MEATBALLS

2 tablespoons olive oil

1 medium leek (350g), sliced thinly

500g chicken mince

1 egg

1 clove garlic, crushed

¾ cup (50g) stale breadcrumbs

1 tablespoon finely chopped fresh tarragon

1   Combine the water, chicken bones, carrot, celery, chopped onion, bay leaf, parsley and peppercorns in large saucepan; bring to a boil. Reduce heat; simmer, uncovered, 2½ hours. Strain stock through muslin-lined sieve or colander into large bowl; discard solids. (Can be made ahead to this stage. Cover; refrigerate overnight.) Return stock to same cleaned pan with wine; bring to a boil. Reduce heat; simmer, covered.

2   Heat oil and butter in large saucepan; cook sliced onion and fennel, stirring, over low heat about 15 minutes or until vegetables soften and are browned lightly.

3   Meanwhile, make chicken meatballs.

4   Add rice and garlic to pan with vegetables; stir to coat in butter mixture. Stir in 1 cup of the simmering stock mixture; cook, stirring, over low heat until liquid is absorbed. Continue adding stock mixture, in 1-cup batches, stirring, until liquid is absorbed after each addition. Total cooking time should be about 35 minutes or until rice is just tender. Gently stir chicken meatballs, cheese and half of the tarragon into risotto; serve sprinkled with remaining tarragon.

CHICKEN MEATBALLS Heat half of the oil in large frying pan; cook leek, stirring, about 5 minutes or until softened. Place leek with remaining ingredients in medium bowl; using hands, mix until combined. Roll level tablespoons of the mixture into balls. Heat remaining oil in same frying pan; cook meatballs, shaking pan occasionally, until browned all over and cooked through.

PER SERVING 24.8g fat; 3195kJ (763 cal)

turkey and lemon risotto

preparation time 10 minutes cooking time 40 minutes serves 6

8 cups (2 litres) chicken stock

1 cup (250ml) dry white wine

½ cup (125ml) lemon juice

2 teaspoons low-fat dairy-free spread

1 medium brown onion (150g), chopped finely

2 cloves garlic, crushed

4 cups (800g) arborio rice

1½ cups (185g) frozen peas

6 turkey fillets (650g)

2 teaspoons finely grated lemon rind

2 teaspoons finely chopped fresh thyme

¼ cup (20g) finely grated parmesan cheese

1 Combine stock, wine and juice in large saucepan; bring to a boil. Reduce heat; simmer, uncovered.
2 Heat dairy-free spread in separate large saucepan; cook onion and garlic, stirring, until onion softens. Add rice; stir to coat in spread mixture. Stir in 1 cup of the hot stock mixture; cook, stirring, over low heat until liquid is absorbed. Continue adding stock mixture, in 1-cup batches, stirring until absorbed between each addition. Add peas; cook 5 minutes. Total cooking time should be about 35 minutes.
3 Meanwhile, cook turkey, in batches, in large oiled frying pan until browned both sides and cooked through; chop coarsely.
4 Gently stir turkey, rind, thyme and cheese into risotto.
   PER SERVING 7.4g fat; 2943kJ (703 cal)

TIP Chicken breast fillets can be substituted for turkey fillets.

gremolata fish on pumpkin risotto

preparation time 30 minutes (plus standing time) cooking time 40 minutes serves 4

750g piece pumpkin

2 tablespoons vegetable oil

2 teaspoons garam masala

2 tablespoons olive oil

1 small brown onion (80g), sliced thinly

1 clove garlic, crushed

2 cups (400g) arborio rice

4 cups (1 litre) chicken stock

100g baby spinach leaves

GREMOLATA FISH

⅓ cup finely chopped fresh flat-leaf parsley

1 tablespoon vegetable oil

1 teaspoon finely grated lemon rind

2 cloves garlic, crushed

4 small white fish fillets (600g)

1 Preheat oven to 240°C/220°C fan-forced.
2 Peel pumpkin, cut into 3cm pieces. Combine pumpkin, vegetable oil and garam masala in large baking dish. Bake, uncovered, in oven about 15 minutes or until pumpkin is browned and just tender.
3 Meanwhile, heat olive oil in large saucepan; cook onion and garlic, stirring, until onion is soft. Add rice, stir to coat in oil mixture. Add stock; bring to a boil. Reduce heat; simmer, covered, 15 minutes, stirring midway through cooking. Remove pan from heat; stand, covered, 10 minutes. Gently stir in pumpkin and spinach; stand, covered, 2 minutes. Serve topped with gremolata fish.
   GREMOLATA FISH Combine parsley, oil, rind and garlic in medium bowl; press onto fish fillets. Cook fish in heated oiled large frying pan until browned both sides and just cooked through.
   PER SERVING 28.8g fat; 3434kJ (821 cal)

saltimbocca with risotto milanese

preparation time 10 minutes cooking time 50 minutes serves 4

8 veal steaks (680g)

4 slices prosciutto (60g), halved crossways

8 fresh sage leaves

½ cup (50g) finely grated pecorino cheese

40g butter

1 cup (250ml) dry white wine

1 tablespoon coarsely chopped fresh sage

RISOTTO MILANESE

1½ cups (375ml) water

2 cups (500ml) chicken stock

½ cup (125ml) dry white wine

¼ teaspoon saffron threads

20g butter

1 large brown onion (200g), chopped finely

2 cups (400g) arborio rice

¼ cup (20g) finely grated parmesan cheese

1 Place steaks on board. Place one piece prosciutto, one sage leaf and ⅛ of the cheese on each steak; fold in half to secure filling, secure with a toothpick or small skewer.

2 Make risotto milanese.

3 Melt half of the butter in medium frying pan; cook saltimbocca, in batches, about 5 minutes or until browned both sides and cooked through. Cover to keep warm.

4 Pour wine into same frying pan; bring to a boil. Boil, uncovered, until wine reduces by half. Stir in remaining butter then chopped sage.

5 Divide risotto milanese and saltimbocca among serving plates; drizzle saltimbocca with sauce and accompany with steamed green beans, if desired.

RISOTTO MILANESE Place the water, stock, wine and saffron in medium saucepan; bring to a boil. Reduce heat; simmer, covered. Heat butter in another medium saucepan; cook onion, stirring, until softened. Add rice; stir to coat rice in onion mixture. Stir in ½ cup of the simmering stock mixture; cook, stirring, over low heat, until liquid is absorbed. Continue adding stock mixture, in ½-cup batches, stirring until absorbed after each addition. Total cooking time should be about 35 minutes or until rice is just tender. Stir cheese gently into risotto.

PER SERVING 23.3g fat; 3429kJ (819 cal)

roasted eye fillet with red wine risotto

preparation time 15 minutes **cooking time** 40 minutes (plus standing time) **serves** 4

500g piece eye fillet

1 tablespoon olive oil

1 teaspoon ground black pepper

¼ cup (60ml) dry red wine

½ cup (125ml) beef stock

RED WINE RISOTTO

3 cups (750ml) vegetable stock

40g butter

1 medium brown onion (150g), chopped finely

1 cup (200g) arborio rice

1 cup (250ml) dry red wine

¼ cup (20g) finely grated parmesan cheese

3 green onions, sliced thinly

1 Preheat oven to 200°C/180°C fan-forced.

2 Trim excess fat from fillet; tie fillet with kitchen string at 3cm intervals. Place fillet in oiled shallow flameproof baking dish; brush all over with oil, sprinkle with pepper. Roast, uncovered, in oven about 20 minutes or until cooked as desired.

3 Meanwhile, start making red wine risotto.

4 Remove fillet from dish, cover; stand 10 minutes. Place baking dish over low heat, add wine; simmer, stirring, about 2 minutes or until mixture reduces by half. Add stock; stir until sauce comes to a boil. Strain sauce into small jug. Serve sliced fillet with red wine risotto, drizzled with sauce.

RED WINE RISOTTO Place stock in medium saucepan; bring to a boil. Reduce heat; simmer, covered. Heat half of the butter in large saucepan; cook brown onion, stirring, until softened. Add rice; stir to coat rice in onion mixture. Add wine; bring to a boil. Reduce heat; simmer, stirring, 2 minutes. Stir in ½ cup of the simmering stock; cook, stirring, over low heat, until liquid is absorbed. Continue adding stock mixture, in ½-cup batches, stirring until absorbed after each addition. Total cooking time should be about 35 minutes or until rice is just tender. Add cheese, remaining butter and green onion, stirring until butter melts.

PER SERVING *23.2g fat; 2397kJ (573 cal)*

TIP This risotto is quite thick and creamy; if this is not to your taste, stir in a little boiling water just before serving.

risotto marinara

preparation time 10 minutes cooking time 25 minutes serves 4

60g butter

1 small brown onion (80g), sliced thinly

2 cloves garlic, crushed

2 cups (400g) arborio rice

4 cups (1 litre) chicken stock

½ cup (125ml) dry white wine

700g seafood marinara mix

1 tablespoon finely grated lemon rind

¼ cup (60ml) lemon juice

¼ cup coarsely chopped fresh dill

¼ cup coarsely chopped fresh flat-leaf parsley

4 green onions, sliced thinly

1 Place half of the butter, onion and garlic in large microwave-safe dish; cook, uncovered, on HIGH (100%) about 2 minutes or until onion softens. Add rice, stir to coat in butter mixture; cook, uncovered, on HIGH (100%) 1 minute. Stir in stock and wine; cook, uncovered, on HIGH (100%) for 15 minutes, pausing to stir every 3 minutes.

2 Stir in marinara mix; cook, uncovered, on HIGH (100%) about 7 minutes or until seafood is changed in colour and rice is just tender, stirring once during cooking. Stir in remaining ingredients and remaining butter just before serving.

PER SERVING 16.7g fat; 2986kJ (713 cal)

spinach and leek risotto

preparation time 10 minutes cooking time 40 minutes serves 4

½ cup (125ml) dry white wine

4 cups (1 litre) vegetable stock

2 cups (500ml) water

80g butter

1 medium leek (350g), sliced thinly

2 cloves garlic, crushed

2 cups (400g) arborio rice

180g baby spinach leaves

½ teaspoon ground nutmeg

1 cup (80g) finely grated parmesan cheese

1 Combine wine, stock and the water in medium saucepan; bring to a boil. Reduce heat; simmer, covered.

2 Meanwhile, melt 60g of the butter in large saucepan; cook leek and garlic, stirring, until leek softens. Add rice; stir to coat in leek mixture. Stir in 1 cup of the simmering stock mixture; cook, stirring, over low heat until liquid is absorbed. Continue adding simmering stock mixture, in 1-cup batches, stirring, until liquid is absorbed after each addition. Total cooking time should be about 35 minutes or until rice is tender. Gently stir in spinach, nutmeg, cheese and remaining butter.

PER SERVING 24.8g fat; 2744kJ (656 cal)

TIP Risotto should be creamy; if it's too thick, you can add a little boiling water.

slow-roasted shanks with pumpkin and carrot risotto

preparation time 30 minutes cooking time 2 hours 45 minutes serves 6

1 large beef shank (2.5kg), quartered crossways

2 tablespoons plain flour

2 tablespoons olive oil

2 x 425g cans crushed tomatoes

½ cup (125ml) dry white wine

½ cup (125ml) beef stock

¼ cup (70g) tomato paste

¼ cup finely chopped fresh flat-leaf parsley

2 tablespoons finely chopped fresh lemon thyme

PUMPKIN AND CARROT RISOTTO

450g butternut pumpkin, chopped coarsely

2 large carrots (360g), chopped coarsely

2 tablespoons olive oil

6 cups (1.5 litres) chicken stock

1 cup (250ml) dry white wine

30g butter

1 medium brown onion (150g), chopped coarsely

2 cups (400g) arborio rice

¼ cup (20g) coarsely grated parmesan cheese

1 Preheat oven to 240°/220°C fan-forced. Roast vegetables for risotto; when vegetables are just tender, remove from oven. Reduce oven temperature to 180°C/160°C fan-forced.

2 Meanwhile, toss shank pieces in flour; shake away excess. Heat oil in large frying pan; cook shank pieces, in batches, until browned and almost crunchy all over.

3 Place undrained tomatoes, wine, stock and paste in deep 5-litre (20 cup) baking dish; stir to combine. Place shank pieces, one at a time, standing upright, in dish; cook, covered, in oven about 2 hours or until tender.

4 Remove shanks from dish. When cool enough to handle, remove meat from bones. Discard bones; chop meat coarsely. Return meat to dish with tomato sauce; reheat if necessary. Stir in herbs just before serving with risotto.

PUMPKIN AND CARROT RISOTTO Place pumpkin and carrot in lightly oiled large shallow baking dish, in single layer; drizzle with oil. Roast, uncovered, in very hot (240°/220°C fan-forced) oven about 20 minutes or until vegetables are just tender. Remove from oven; reserve. About 40 minutes before shanks are cooked, place stock and wine in medium saucepan; bring to a boil. Reduce heat; simmer, covered. Melt butter in large saucepan; cook onion, stirring, until softened. Add rice; stir to coat in onion mixture. Stir in 1 cup of the hot stock mixture; cook, stirring, over low heat, until liquid is absorbed. Continue adding stock mixture, in 1-cup batches, stirring until absorbed after each addition. Gently stir pumpkin, carrot and cheese into risotto with last cup of stock mixture. Total cooking time should be about 35 minutes or until rice is just tender.

PER SERVING 36.5g fat; 3693kJ (882 cal)

veal braciole with rice and peas

preparation time 25 minutes **cooking time** 40 minutes **serves** 4

The Italian veal cut known as braciole is similar to a schnitzel or scallop, a thinly sliced piece cut from the leg and fairly free of fat. It must be browned quickly to avoid excessive shrinkage and toughness.

8 slices pancetta (120g)

8 veal schnitzels (800g)

²/₃ cup (100g) drained sun-dried tomatoes in oil, sliced thinly

⅓ cup (55g) seeded green olives, sliced thinly

1 tablespoon drained baby capers, rinsed

2 teaspoons fresh marjoram leaves

1 tablespoon olive oil

RICE AND PEAS

4 cups (1 litre) water

2 cups (500ml) chicken stock

40g butter

2 cups (400g) arborio rice

1 cup (125g) frozen baby peas

1 cup (80g) finely grated parmesan cheese

¼ cup finely chopped fresh flat-leaf parsley

1 Preheat oven to 180°C/160°C fan-forced.

2 Place one slice of pancetta on each schnitzel; divide tomato, olives, capers and marjoram between schnitzels.

3 Roll schnitzels to enclose filling; tie with kitchen string to secure.

4 Start making rice and peas.

5 Heat oil in large frying pan; cook braciole, uncovered, until browned all over. Place on oven tray; bake, uncovered, in oven about 10 minutes or until cooked through.

6 Serve braciole with rice and peas.
   RICE AND PEAS Place the water and stock in medium saucepan; bring to a boil. Reduce heat; simmer, covered. Melt butter in large saucepan, add rice; stir until rice is coated in butter and slightly opaque. Stir in 1 cup of the hot stock mixture; cook, stirring, over low heat, until liquid is absorbed. Continue adding stock mixture, in 1-cup batches, stirring until absorbed after each addition. Add peas with last cup of stock mixture; stir in cheese and parsley.
   PER SERVING *30.4g fat; 3938kJ (941 cal)*

pork, pine nut and cointreau risotto

preparation time 25 minutes (plus standing time) cooking time 20 minutes serves 4

500g pork fillets

1 tablespoon teriyaki marinade

1 teaspoon finely grated orange rind

3 cloves garlic, crushed

1 large brown onion (200g), chopped finely

2 cups (400g) arborio rice

5 cups (1.25 litres) chicken stock

½ cup (125ml) dry white wine

2 tablespoons Cointreau

150g baby spinach leaves

2 tablespoons pine nuts, toasted

2 tablespoons coarsely chopped fresh lemon thyme

1 Preheat oven to 220°C/200°C fan-forced.

2 Place pork on rack in baking dish; brush with combined marinade and rind. Bake, uncovered, in oven 20 minutes. Cover pork, stand 5 minutes; slice thinly.

3 Meanwhile, cook garlic and onion in heated, oiled large pan, stirring, until onion softens. Add rice, stock, wine and Cointreau, bring to boil, simmer, covered, 15 minutes, stirring midway through cooking. Remove from heat, stand, covered, 10 minutes. Gently stir in spinach, pine nuts, thyme and pork.
PER SERVE *7.6g fat; 2572kJ (615 cal)*

prawn and asparagus risotto

preparation time 30 minutes cooking time 50 minutes serves 6

32 uncooked medium prawns (approximately 1kg)

500g fresh asparagus

6 cups (1.5 litres) chicken stock

1½ cups (375ml) dry white wine

30g butter

1 large brown onion (200g), chopped finely

2 cloves garlic, crushed

3 cups (600g) arborio rice

2 medium tomatoes (380g), seeded, chopped finely

⅓ cup loosely packed, coarsely chopped fresh flat-leaf parsley

½ teaspoon cracked black pepper

1 Shell and devein prawns, leaving tails intact. Slice asparagus diagonally into 3cm lengths.

2 Combine stock and wine in large saucepan. Bring to a boil; cover. Reduce heat; simmer to keep hot.

3 Melt butter in large saucepan; cook onion and garlic, stirring, until onion is soft. Add rice; stir to coat in butter mixture. Stir in 1 cup of the hot stock mixture; cook, stirring, over low heat until liquid is absorbed. Continue adding stock mixture, in 1-cup batches, stirring, until liquid is absorbed after each addition. Total cooking time should be about 35 minutes or until rice is just tender.

4 Add prawns, asparagus, tomato, parsley and pepper; cook, stirring, until prawns are just changed in colour and asparagus is tender.
PER SERVING *5.6g fat; 2444kJ (584 cal)*

TIP If arborio rice is unavailable, use the shortest, most round-grain white rice you can find. Long-grained rice will always remain as individual grains, never absorbing enough liquid to achieve the proper soupy-soft texture of a perfect risotto.

blackened ocean trout fillets with burnt-butter risotto

preparation time 25 minutes cooking time 45 minutes serves 4

1 teaspoon sweet paprika

1 tablespoon dried thyme

1 tablespoon dried oregano

1 teaspoon cayenne pepper

2 teaspoons garlic powder

4 x 220g ocean trout fillets, with skin

BURNT-BUTTER RISOTTO

2 cups (500ml) water

2 cups (500ml) vegetable stock

80g butter

1 tablespoon olive oil

1 cup (250ml) dry white wine

1 medium brown onion (150g), chopped finely

1 clove garlic, crushed

1¼ cups (250g) arborio rice

¼ cup finely chopped fresh flat-leaf parsley

¼ cup (20g) finely grated parmesan cheese

1   Combine spices, herbs and garlic powder in medium bowl; using fingers, press spice mixture into skin-side of fish fillets. Cover fish; refrigerate.

2   Meanwhile, make burnt-butter risotto.

3   Cook fish in large oiled frying pan, skin-side up, until browned lightly. Turn; cook fish until skin browns and fish is cooked as desired. Serve fish, skin-side up, on risotto.

BURNT-BUTTER RISOTTO Combine the water and stock in medium saucepan; bring to a boil. Reduce heat; simmer, covered. Heat butter and oil in large saucepan until butter begins to brown slightly. Add wine; cook until liquid reduces by half. Add onion and garlic; cook, stirring, until onion softens. Add rice; stir to coat in onion mixture. Stir in ½ cup of the simmering stock; cook, stirring, over low heat, until liquid is absorbed. Continue adding stock, in ½-cup batches, stirring, until liquid is absorbed between each addition. Total cooking time should be about 35 minutes or until rice is tender. Stir in parsley and cheese.

PER SERVING *33g fat; 3205kJ (766 cal)*

scampi and fennel risotto

preparation time 30 minutes cooking time 1 hour serves 4

2kg uncooked scampi

1 large fennel (550g)

¼ teaspoon black peppercorns

1 large brown onion (200g), quartered

1 trimmed celery stick (75g), chopped coarsely

6½ cups (1.625 litres) water

1½ cups (375ml) fish stock

40g butter

2 tablespoons olive oil

2 cloves garlic, crushed

2 cups (400g) arborio rice

1 cup (250ml) dry white wine

2 tablespoons coarsely chopped fresh chervil

1 Remove heads from scampi; discard contents, wash and reserve head shells. Cut through tails lengthways. Discard back vein from tail; remove and reserve meat.

2 Remove and reserve fennel stalks and green tips; halve and slice fennel bulb thinly, reserve.

3 Place head shells, fennel stalks and green tips, peppercorns, onion and celery in large saucepan with the water and fish stock; bring to a boil. Reduce heat; simmer, uncovered, 10 minutes. Strain stock into large heatproof bowl; discard solids. Return stock to same saucepan; bring to a boil. Reduce heat; simmer, covered.

4 Heat half of the butter with oil in large heavy-based saucepan; cook garlic and reserved fennel, stirring, until fennel softens. Add rice; stir to coat rice in butter mixture. Add wine; stir until wine reduces by half. Stir in 1 cup simmering stock; cook, stirring, over low heat until liquid is absorbed. Continue adding stock, in 1-cup batches, stirring until liquid is absorbed after each addition. Total cooking time should be about 35 minutes or until rice is just tender.

5 Add remaining butter and reserved scampi meat to risotto; stir gently to combine. Stir in chervil just before serving.
PER SERVING *19.4g fat; 2961kJ (707 cal)*

oven-baked risotto with chicken, rocket and semi-dried tomato

preparation time 10 minutes cooking time 35 minutes serves 4

1 tablespoon olive oil

1 large brown onion (200g), sliced thinly

2 cloves garlic, crushed

2 cups (400g) arborio rice

¾ cup (180ml) dry white wine

4 cups (1 litre) chicken stock

4 single chicken breast fillets (680g)

100g baby rocket leaves

100g semi-dried tomatoes, sliced thinly

½ cup (40g) finely grated parmesan cheese

1 tablespoon coarsely chopped fresh flat-leaf parsley

1   Preheat oven to 180°C/160°C fan-forced.
2   Heat oil in shallow 3-litre (12-cup) flameproof baking dish; cook onion and garlic, stirring, until onion softens. Add rice; stir to coat in onion mixture. Stir in wine and stock; bring to a boil. Place chicken, in single layer, on top of rice mixture. Transfer dish to oven; bake, covered, about 25 minutes or until rice is tender and chicken is cooked through. Remove chicken; stand chicken 5 minutes. Slice thickly.
3   Stir rocket, tomato and a third of the cheese into risotto; serve risotto topped with chicken. Sprinkle remaining cheese and parsley over chicken.
    PER SERVING *21.3g fat; 3414kJ (815 cal)*

seafood risotto

preparation time 30 minutes cooking time 30 minutes serves 4

30 uncooked medium prawns (750g)

2 tablespoons olive oil

1 medium brown onion (150g), chopped finely

2 cups (400g) arborio rice

3½ cups (875ml) hot vegetable stock

500g seafood marinara mix

½ cup (125ml) cream

½ cup (40g) coarsely grated parmesan cheese

¼ cup chopped fresh flat-leaf parsley

1   Shell and devein prawns, cut in half lengthways.
2   Combine oil and onion in large microwave-safe dish; cook, uncovered, on HIGH (100%) 4 minutes, stirring once during cooking. Stir in rice; cook, uncovered, on HIGH (100%) 1 minute.
3   Add stock; cook, covered, on HIGH (100%) 10 minutes, stirring twice during cooking.
4   Stir in all seafood; cook, covered, on MEDIUM (55%) about 6 minutes or until seafood has changed in colour and rice is just tender, stirring once during cooking.
5   Stir in cream and cheese; cook, covered, on MEDIUM (55%) 3 minutes. Stand, covered, 5 minutes; stir in parsley.
    PER SERVING *30.2g fat; 3437kJ (821 cal)*

vodka mussels with lemon dill risotto

preparation time 15 minutes cooking time 45 minutes serves 4

2 tablespoons olive oil

2 small brown onions (160g), chopped finely

1½ cups (300g) arborio rice

4 cups (1 litre) hot vegetable stock

2 cloves garlic, crushed

2 red thai chillies, chopped finely

⅓ cup coarsely chopped fresh parsley stems

⅓ cup (80ml) vodka

24 medium black mussels (600g)

2 tablespoons finely grated lemon rind

2 tablespoons finely chopped fresh dill

1 Heat half of the oil in large pan; cook half of the onion, stirring, until soft. Add rice; stir to coat in oil mixture. Stir in 1 cup stock; cook, stirring, over low heat until liquid is absorbed. Continue adding stock in 1-cup batches, stirring until absorbed before next addition. Total cooking time should be about 35 minutes or until rice is just tender.

2 Meanwhile, scrub mussels and remove beards. Heat remaining oil in medium pan; cook remaining onion, garlic and chilli, stirring, until onion is soft. Stir in parsley and vodka; cook, stirring, 2 minutes. Stir in mussels; cook, covered, about 10 minutes or until mussels open. Discard any mussels that do not open.

3 Drain mussels over medium heatproof bowl; reserve liquid. Pick out mussels, shake off cooking solids, place mussels in medium bowl. Stir reserved liquid into risotto; cook risotto, stirring, until liquid is absorbed.

4 Stir rind and dill into risotto; serve with mussels.
   PER SERVING *14g fat; 1848kJ (442 cal)*

   TIP If arborio rice is unavailable, some other types of short-grain rice are suitable for risotto.

garlic prawns with herbed rice

preparation time 20 minutes **cooking time** 15 minutes **serves** 6

36 uncooked medium prawns (1kg)

6 cloves garlic, crushed

2 teaspoons finely chopped fresh coriander

3 fresh red thai chillies, seeded, chopped finely

⅓ cup (80ml) lime juice

1 teaspoon white sugar

1 tablespoon peanut oil

1kg baby buk choy, quartered lengthways

6 green onions, sliced thinly

1 tablespoon sweet chilli sauce

HERBED RICE

2 cups (400g) jasmine rice

2 tablespoons chopped fresh coriander

1 tablespoon chopped fresh mint

1 tablespoon chopped fresh flat-leaf parsley

1 teaspoon finely grated lime rind

1 Shell and devein prawns, leaving tails intact.
2 Combine prawns in large bowl with garlic, coriander, chilli, juice and sugar.
3 Heat half of the oil in wok or large frying pan; stir-fry prawns, in batches, until just changed in colour.
4 Heat remaining oil with pan liquids in wok; stir-fry buk choy, onion and sauce, in batches, until just tender. Combine buk choy mixture and prawns in wok; stir-fry until hot. Serve prawns on herbed rice.

HERBED RICE Cook rice, uncovered, in large saucepan of boiling water until tender; drain. Return rice to pan; combine with remaining ingredients.

PER SERVING *4.5g fat; 1602kJ (383 cal)*

SEAFOOD

lime and chilli fish with jasmine rice

preparation time 25 minutes cooking time 15 minutes serves 8

2 large banana leaves

4 stalks lemon grass

4 fresh red thai chillies, seeded, sliced thinly

4 cloves garlic, crushed

1 tablespoon finely grated lime rind

⅓ cup (80ml) lime juice

2 tablespoons grated fresh ginger

1 cup chopped fresh coriander

1 cup (250ml) light coconut milk

8 x 150g ling fillets

cooking-oil spray

2 cups (400g) jasmine rice

4 green onions, sliced thinly

1 Preheat oven to 220°C/200°C fan-forced.

2 Trim each banana leaf into four 30cm squares. Using metal tongs, dip one square at a time into large saucepan of boiling water; remove immediately. Rinse under cold running water; pat dry with absorbent paper. Banana leaf squares should be soft and pliable.

3 Halve lemon grass stalks. Combine chilli, garlic, rind, juice, ginger, coriander and coconut milk in small bowl.

4 Centre each fish fillet on banana leaf square. Top with lemon grass; drizzle with chilli mixture. Fold square over fish to enclose; secure each parcel with kitchen string.

5 Place parcels, in single layer, in large baking dish; coat with cooking-oil spray. Roast in oven about 10 minutes or until fish is cooked as desired.

6 Meanwhile, cook rice, uncovered, in large saucepan of boiling water until tender; drain. Stir onion through rice; serve with unwrapped fish parcels.

PER SERVING *7g fat; 1592kJ (381 cal)*

TIP Many supermarkets and greengrocers sell bundles of trimmed banana-leaf squares; they can also be used as placemats for an Asian meal. Use foil to wrap fish if banana leaves are unavailable.

sushi rice

preparation time 10 minutes (plus draining time) **cooking time** 12 minutes (plus standing time) **makes** 9 cups

3 cups (600g) short-grain white rice

3 cups (750ml) water

SUSHI VINEGAR

½ cup (125ml) rice vinegar

¼ cup (55g) white sugar

½ teaspoon salt

1　Place rice in large bowl, fill with cold water, stir with hand. Drain; repeat process two or three times until water is almost clear. Drain rice in strainer or colander at least 30 minutes.

2　Meanwhile, prepare sushi vinegar.

3　To cook rice in rice cooker: place drained rice and the water in rice cooker, cover; switch onto "cook". When cooker automatically switches to "keep warm" position, allow rice to stand, covered, 10 minutes. To cook rice in saucepan: place drained rice and the water in medium saucepan, cover tightly; bring to a boil. Reduce heat; simmer, covered tightly, on low heat about 12 minutes or until water is absorbed. Remove from heat; allow rice to stand, covered, 10 minutes.

4　Spread rice in a large, non-metallic flat-bottomed bowl or tub (preferably wood). Using a rice paddle, a large flat woode n spoon or a plastic spatula, repeatedly slice through the rice at a sharp angle to break up lumps and separate grains, gradually pouring in the sushi vinegar at the same time. Not all of the vinegar may be required; the rice shouldn't become too wet or mushy.

5　Continue to slice (don't stir because it crushes the rice grains) with one hand, lifting and turning the rice from the outside into the centre (this action is similar to folding beaten egg whites into a cake mixture).

6　Meanwhile, using the other hand, fan the rice until it is almost cool; this will take about 5 minutes (an electric fan, on the low setting, can be used instead of a hand-held fan if you prefer). Do not over-cool rice or it will harden. Performing these two actions together will give you glossy, slightly sticky but still separate sushi rice. Keep the rice covered with a damp cloth to stop it drying out while making sushi.

SUSHI VINEGAR Stir combined vinegar, sugar and salt in small bowl until sugar dissolves. To make this mixture slightly less stringent, heat it gently just before using.

TIP You can add either a little mirin or sake to the sushi vinegar mixture if you like, or you can use ½ cup (125ml) ready-made bottled sushi vinegar. Sushi vinegar can be made ahead and refrigerated in an airtight container.

tuna rolls

preparation time 20 minutes **makes** 6 rolls (36 pieces)

3 sheets toasted seaweed (yaki-nori)

medium bowl filled with cold water, with
1 tablespoon rice vinegar added

3 cups prepared sushi rice (see page 70)

1 tablespoon wasabi

200g piece sashimi tuna, cut into 1cm-thick strips

2 tablespoons pink pickled ginger (gari)

¼ cup (60ml) soy sauce

1 Fold one sheet of seaweed in half lengthways, parallel with lines marked on rough side of seaweed; cut along fold. Place a half sheet, shiny-side down, lengthways across bamboo mat about 2cm from edge of mat closest to you.

2 Dip fingers in bowl of vinegared water; shake off excess. Pick up about ½ cup of the rice, squeeze into oblong shape, and place across centre of seaweed sheet.

3 Wet fingers again, then, working from left to right, gently "rake" rice evenly over seaweed, leaving 2cm strip on far end of seaweed uncovered. Build up rice in front of uncovered seaweed strip to form mound to keep filling in place.

4 Using finger, swipe a dab of wasabi across centre of rice, flattening it out evenly.

5 Place tuna strips, end to end, in a row over wasabi across centre of rice.

6 Starting with edge closest to you, pick up mat, using thumb and index fingers of both hands; use remaining fingers to hold filling in place as you begin to roll mat away from you. Roll forward, pressing gently but tightly, wrapping seaweed around rice and fillings.

7 When roll is completed, a strip of uncovered seaweed will stick to the bottom of the roll to form join; exert gentle pressure to make the roll slightly square in shape.

8 Unroll mat; place sushi roll, join-down, on board. Wipe very sharp knife with damp cloth then cut roll in half. Turn one half piece around 180 degrees so that the two cut ends of each half are aligned. Slice through both rolls together twice, to give a total of six bite-sized pieces, wiping knife between each cut.

9 Working quickly, repeat process with remaining seaweed halves, rice and tuna, using a dab of wasabi with each. Serve tuna rolls with remaining wasabi, pickled ginger and sauce served separately.
PER PIECE *0.4g fat; 130kJ (31 cal)*

inside-out rolls

preparation time 20 minutes **makes** 4 rolls (32 pieces)

2 sheets toasted seaweed (yaki-nori), folded parallel with lines on rough side of seaweed, cut in half

medium bowl filled with cold water, with 1 tablespoon rice vinegar added

4 cups prepared sushi rice (see page 70)

2 tablespoons flying fish roe

1 teaspoon toasted black sesame seeds

1½ tablespoons wasabi

½ lebanese cucumber (65g), halved, seeded, sliced thinly

4 cooked large prawns (200g), shelled, deveined, halved lengthways

4 strips 5mm x 18cm pickled daikon (takuan)

1½ tablespoons red pickled ginger (beni-shoga)

2 tablespoons pink pickled ginger (gari)

¼ cup (60ml) soy sauce

1 Place one half-sheet seaweed lengthways across bamboo mat about 2cm from edge of mat closest to you. Dip fingers of one hand in bowl of vinegared water, shake off excess; pick up a quarter of the rice, press onto seaweed then, working from left to right, gently "rake" rice to cover seaweed completely and evenly.

2 Sprinkle a quarter of the roe and seeds over rice then cover rice completely with a piece of plastic wrap. Carefully lift mat; turn over so seaweed faces up; place back on bamboo mat about 2cm from the edge. Using finger, swipe a dab of wasabi across centre of seaweed, then top with about a quarter of the cucumber, prawn, pickled daikon and red pickled ginger, making certain that filling extends to both ends of seaweed.

3 Pick up the edge of the bamboo mat and plastic wrap with index finger and thumb; place remaining fingers on filling to hold in place as you roll mat tightly away from you, wrapping rice around filling. Press roll gently and continue rolling forward to complete the roll. Unroll mat and keep roll in plastic wrap.

4 Wipe sharp knife with damp cloth; cut roll, still in plastic wrap, in half, then each half into quarters, to make eight pieces, wiping knife between each cut. Remove plastic wrap and serve inside-out rolls with remaining wasabi, pink pickled ginger and sauce.
PER PIECE *0.3g fat; 238kJ (57 cal)*

TIPS Make two small cuts in the underside of the prawns so they lie flat. Keep finished inside-out rolls wrapped in plastic wrap, uncut, until ready to serve to prevent them from drying out.

SEAFOOD

hand-moulded sushi

preparation time 20 minutes makes 30

medium bowl filled with cold water, with 1 tablespo on rice vinegar added

3 cups prepared sushi rice (see page 70)

350g sashimi tuna, sliced thinly

2 teaspoons wasabi

¼ cup (60ml) soy sauce

1 Dip fingers of both hands in bowl of vinegared water, shake off excess; pick up about 1 tablespoon of rice with your right hand, gently squeezing and shaping it into a rectangle shape with rounded edges.

2 Pick up one slice of fish with the index finger and thumb of the left hand. Using tip of right-hand index finger, scoop up a dab of wasabi; spread wasabi along centre of fish.

3 Bend fingers of left hand to form cup to hold fish; place rice shape on fish.

4 Move left thumb to top end of rice shape to stop rice being pushed off fish; use right-hand index and middle fingers to gently push rice shape and fish together.

5 Turn sushi piece over so fish is on top, gently push fish against rice with right-hand index and middle fingers; left thumb should remain at top end of rice to stop it being pushed out.

6 With thumb on one side of rice and index finger on the other, gently squeeze rice to straighten the sides.

7 Using right-hand index finger and thumb, turn sushi 180 degrees and push fish against rice again with right-hand index and middle fingers.

8 Serve hand-moulded sushi with sauce in a separate bowl.
   PER PIECE *0.7g fat; 117kJ (28 cal)*

crab fried rice in omelette

preparation time 15 minutes **cooking time** 25 minutes **serves** 4

You need to cook ⅔ cup of jasmine rice the day before making this recipe.

¼ cup (60ml) peanut oil

4 green onions, chopped finely

2 fresh small red thai chillies, chopped finely

1 tablespoon red curry paste

2 cups cooked jasmine rice

250g fresh crab meat

2 tablespoons lime juice

2 tablespoons fish sauce

8 eggs

2 tablespoons water

1 lime, cut into wedges

1 Heat 1 tablespoon of the oil in wok; stir-fry onion and chopped chilli until onion softens. Add curry paste; stir-fry until mixture is fragrant.

2 Add rice; stir-fry until heated through. Remove from heat; place in large bowl. Add crab meat, juice and sauce; toss to combine.

3 Whisk eggs with the water in medium bowl. Heat about a quarter of the remaining oil in same cleaned wok; pour a quarter of the egg mixture into wok. Cook, tilting pan, over low heat until almost set. Spoon a quarter of the fried rice into centre of the omelette; using spatula, fold four sides of omelette over to enclose filling.

4 Press omelette firmly with spatula; turn carefully to brown other side. Remove omelette from wok; cover to keep warm. Repeat process with remaining oil, egg mixture and fried rice. Place omelettes on serving plate; serve with lime.

PER SERVING *26.3g fat; 1599kJ (382 cal)*

sushi salad

preparation time 25 minutes **cooking time** 15 minutes **serves** 4

Koshihikari rice is grown locally from Japanese seed. You can substitute a white medium-grain rice if it's unavailable.

2 cups (400g) koshihikari rice

2 cups (500ml) water

2 lebanese cucumbers (260g)

½ small daikon (200g)

1 lemon, unpeeled, quartered, sliced thinly

400g piece sashimi salmon, sliced thinly

¼ cup (35g) toasted sesame seeds

1 sheet toasted seaweed (yaki-nori), shredded finely

MIRIN AND WASABI DRESSING

4cm piece fresh ginger (20g), grated

2 tablespoons mirin

1 teaspoon wasabi paste

1 tablespoon soy sauce

⅓ cup (80ml) water

¼ cup (60ml) rice wine vinegar

1　Rinse rice in strainer under cold water until water runs clear. Place drained rice and the water in medium saucepan, cover tightly; bring to a boil. Reduce heat; simmer, covered tightly, about 12 minutes or until water is absorbed and rice is just cooked. Remove from heat; stand rice, covered, 10 minutes.

2　Meanwhile, make mirin and wasabi dressing.

3　Using vegetable peeler, slice cucumbers into ribbons. Slice daikon thinly; cut slices into matchstick-sized pieces. Combine rice, cucumber and daikon in large bowl with lemon, fish, dressing and half of the seeds; toss gently to combine. Divide salad among serving bowls; top with seaweed and remaining seeds.

MIRIN AND WASABI DRESSING Combine ingredients in screw-top jar; shake well.

PER SERVING *13.3g fat; 3078kJ (735 cal)*

TIP The easiest way to shred nori without tearing the delicate sheets is to use kitchen scissors.

SEAFOOD

81

balti biryani

preparation time 25 minutes (plus standing and refrigeration time) cooking time 1 hour 20 minutes serves 4

750g beef skirt steak, cut into 2cm cubes

¾ cup (225g) balti curry paste

2 cups (400g) basmati rice

8 cloves garlic, unpeeled

20g ghee

4 cardamom pods, bruised

4 cloves

1 cinnamon stick

3 green onions, sliced thinly

2 cups (500ml) beef stock

¾ cup (100g) toasted slivered almonds

¼ cup loosely packed fresh coriander leaves

2 fresh small red thai chillies, sliced thinly

1 Preheat oven to 180°C/160°C fan-forced.

2 Combine beef and curry paste in medium bowl, cover; refrigerate 1 hour.

3 Meanwhile, place rice in medium bowl, cover with water; stand 30 minutes. Drain rice in strain er; rinse under cold water, drain.

4 Meanwhile, place garlic in small baking dish; roast, uncovered, in oven about 20 minutes or until softened.

5 Melt ghee in large saucepan; cook cardamom, cloves, cinnamon and onion, stirring, until fragrant. Add beef mixture, reduce heat; simmer, covered, stirring occasionally, about 45 minutes or until beef is tender.

6 Add rice with stock to pan; simmer, covered, stirring occasionally, about 15 minutes or until rice is just tender.

7 Peel garlic; chop finely. Add garlic, nuts and coriander to biryani, cover; stand 5 minutes. Sprinkle biryani with chilli; serve with raita and naan, if desired.

PER SERVING *41.9g fat; 4016kJ (959 cal)*

MEAT

chicken and egg on rice

preparation time 10 minutes (plus standing time) **cooking time** 10 minutes **serves** 4

Koshihikari rice is grown locally from Japanese seed. You can substitute a white medium-grain rice if it's unavailable. You will need 1½ cups (300g) uncooked rice to make 4 cups (600g) hot cooked rice.

4 dried shiitake mushrooms

½ cup (125ml) dashi

¼ cup (60ml) soy sauce

2 tablespoons mirin

1 teaspoon white sugar

100g chicken breast fillet, sliced thinly

1 small leek (200g), sliced thinly

6 eggs, beaten lightly

4 cups (600g) hot cooked koshihikari rice

2 tablespoons finely chopped fresh chives

1 Place mushrooms in small heatproof bowl, cover with boiling water, stand about 20 minutes or until just tender; drain. Discard stems and halve caps.

2 Meanwhile, bring dashi, sauce, mirin and sugar to a boil in large frying pan.

3 Add chicken, leek and mushrooms; cook, covered, about 3 minutes or until chicken is tender.

4 Pour egg over chicken mixture; cook, covered, over low heat for about 2 minutes or until egg just sets.

5 Divide rice among serving bowls; top with chicken mixture, and then sprinkle with chives.
PER SERVING *9.8g fat; 1526kJ (365 cal)*

TIP Egg mixture should be just set, still a little runny in areas. Remove from heat and keep covered to cook egg a little longer, if desired.

oven-baked risotto with italian sausages

preparation time 15 minutes **cooking time** 40 minutes **serves** 6

500g spicy Italian-style sausages

4 cups (1 litre) chicken stock

1 tablespoon olive oil

40g butter

2 large brown onions (400g), chopped coarsely

1 clove garlic, crushed

2 cups (400g) arborio rice

¾ cup (180ml) dry white wine

1 cup (160g) drained semi-dried tomatoes

¼ cup fresh basil leaves

¼ cup (20g) coarsely grated parmesan cheese

1   Preheat oven to 180°C/160°C fan-forced.
2   Heat flameproof dish on stove top; add sausages and cook until browned all over and cooked through. Remove from dish; slice thickly.
3   Meanwhile, add stock to medium saucepan; bring to a boil.
4   Heat oil and butter in same flameproof dish; cook onion and garlic, stirring, until soft. Add rice; stir to coat in the onion mixture. Add wine, bring to a boil then simmer, uncovered, 1 minute. Add stock, sausages and tomatoes; cover with lid and cook in moderate oven about 25 minutes or until liquid is absorbed and rice is tender. Stir once during cooking.
5   Stir in the basil and cheese.
PER SERVING *33.9g fat; 2855kJ (682 cal)*

TIP Recipe is best made close to serving.

beef and rice soup

preparation time 10 minutes **cooking time** 10 minutes **serves** 4

Koshihikari rice is grown locally from Japanese seed. If necessary, you can substitute it with a medium-grain white rice. You will need 1½ cups (300g) uncooked rice to make 4 cups (600g) cooked rice.

5 cups (1.25 litres) dashi

3 teaspoons light soy sauce

4 cups (600g) hot cooked koshihikari rice

150g lean beef fillet, cut into paper-thin slices

2 teaspoons toasted white sesame seeds

2 green onions, chopped finely

1 tablespoon wasabi

1   Bring dashi and sauce to a boil in medium saucepan.
2   Divide hot rice among serving bowls; arrange beef, seeds and onion on top of the rice. Pour equal amounts of hot dashi mixture into bowls, taking care not to dislodge the arrangement; serve immediately with wasabi in individual dishes.
PER SERVING *5g fat; 2633kJ (630 cal)*

TIPS If you place beef, wrapped in plastic wrap, in your freezer for about an hour, it will be easier to slice thinly.
Beef will cook in the hot dashi mixture if sliced very thinly. You can also brown unsliced beef in medium frying pan to add extra flavour.

sweet soy beef on rice

preparation time 10 minutes cooking time 10 minutes serves 4

Ginger juice can be obtained by squeezing grated fresh green (that is, young) ginger into a sieve over a bowl. You will need about 2 tablespoons grated fresh ginger to make 2 teaspoons ginger juice.

200g gelatinous noodles (shirataki), drained

½ cup (125ml) soy sauce

1 tablespoon white sugar

¼ cup (60ml) mirin or sweet white wine

300g beef eye fillet, sliced paper thin

2 green onions, sliced diagonally into 2cm lengths

2 teaspoons fresh ginger juice

5 cups (920g) hot cooked koshihikari rice

1 Place noodles in medium saucepan of boiling water; bring to a boil. Cook 1 minute, separating noodles with chopsticks. Drain noodles, cut into 10cm lengths.

2 Bring sauce, sugar and mirin to a boil in medium saucepan. Add beef; cook, stirring, until beef just changes colour. Strain beef over medium heatproof bowl; return sauce to same saucepan.

3 Add onion and noodles to the pan and simmer about 3 minutes or until onion softens. Return beef to pan, add ginger juice; heat through.

4 Divide rice among serving bowls. Top rice with beef and noodles and about ¼ cup (60ml) of the sauce.
PER SERVING 5.2g fat; 1977kJ (473 cal)

chicken and thai basil fried rice

preparation time 15 minutes cooking time 25 minutes serves 4

You will need to cook about 1⅓ cups (265g) rice for this recipe.

¼ cup (60ml) peanut oil

1 medium brown onion (150g), chopped finely

3 cloves garlic, crushed

2 fresh long green chillies, seeded, chopped finely

1 tablespoon brown sugar

500g chicken breast fillets, chopped coarsely

2 medium red capsicums (400g), sliced thinly

200g green beans, chopped coarsely

4 cups cooked jasmine rice

2 tablespoons fish sauce

2 tablespoons soy sauce

½ cup loosely packed fresh thai basil leaves

1 Heat oil in wok or large frying pan; stir-fry onion, garlic and chilli until onion softens. Add sugar; stir-fry until dissolved. Add chicken; stir-fry until lightly browned. Add capsicum and beans; stir-fry until vegetables are just tender and chicken is cooked through.

2 Add rice and sauces; stir-fry, tossing gently to combine. Remove from heat; add basil leaves, toss gently to combine.
   PER SERVING *21.7g fat; 1922kJ (459 cal)*

apricot chicken with creamy rice

preparation time 10 minutes cooking time 1 hour 25 minutes serves 4

12 chicken drumsticks (1.8kg)

2 tablespoons vegetable oil

2 large brown onions (400g), sliced thickly

2 teaspoons grated fresh ginger

2 cloves garlic, crushed

425g can apricot nectar

1 cup (250ml) water

40g packet French onion soup mix

1 cup (200g) short-grain white rice

1 tablespoon finely chopped flat-leaf fresh parsley

1 Remove and discard skin from chicken.

2 Heat half the oil in large pan; cook chicken, in batches, until browned all over. Drain on absorbent paper.

3 Heat remaining oil in same pan; cook onion, ginger and garlic, stirring, for about 5 minutes or until onion is browned lightly.

4 Return chicken to pan with nectar, the water and dry soup mix; bring to boil. Simmer, covered, 10 minutes.

5 Add the rice; simmer, uncovered, stirring occasionally, about 30 minutes or until rice is tender. Just before serving, gently stir in parsley.
   PER SERVING *4.8g fat; 514kJ (123 cal)*

chicken curry with onion pilau

preparation time 25 minutes (plus standing time) **cooking time** 1 hour 35 minutes **serves** 4

4 chicken thigh cutlets (640g)

4 chicken drumsticks (600g)

⅓ cup (50g) plain flour

1½ tablespoons vegetable oil

2 large brown onions (400g), sliced thickly

2 cloves garlic, crushed

½ teaspoon chilli powder

1 tablespoon ground cumin

⅓ cup (40g) curry powder

2 x 440g cans crushed tomatoes

¼ cup (60ml) tomato paste

1 tablespoon brown sugar

4 cups (1 litre) chicken stock

ONION PILAU

20g butter

2 large brown onions (400g), chopped finely

2 teaspoons cumin seeds

1½ cups (300g) basmati rice

3 cups (750ml) chicken stock

1 Remove skin from chicken pieces; discard skin. Toss chicken in flour, shake off excess.

2 Heat 1 tablespoon of the oil in large pan; cook chicken, in batches, until browned. Drain on absorbent paper.

3 Heat remaining oil in pan; cook onion, garlic, chilli, cumin and curry powder, stirring, until fragrant.

4 Return chicken to pan with the undrained tomatoes, paste, sugar and stock. Bring to boil; simmer, covered, 30 minutes. Simmer, uncovered, about 30 minutes or until chicken is tender. (Can be made ahead to this stage. Cover; refrigerate overnight or freeze.) Serve chicken with the onion pilau.

ONION PILAU Heat butter in medium pan; cook onion and seeds, stirring, until onion is browned lightly. Add rice; cook, stirring, 1 minute. Stir in stock; simmer, covered, about 15 minutes or until rice is just tender. Remove from heat, fluff rice with a fork; stand, covered, 5 minutes.

PER SERVING 28g fat; 3612kJ (864 cal)

chicken and rice salad with nam jim dressing

preparation time 20 minutes cooking time 35 minutes serves 4

4 cups (1 litre) water

600g chicken breast fillets

15cm piece fresh lemon grass

2 star anise

2cm piece fresh ginger (10g), sliced thickly

1 tablespoon peanut oil

1 small brown onion (80g), chopped finely

1 cup (200g) basmati and wild rice mix

300g snow peas, trimmed

1 medium yellow capsicum (200g), sliced thinly

150g mizuna

½ cup firmly packed fresh coriander leaves

NAM JIM DRESSING

10cm piece fresh lemon grass, chopped coarsely

2 cloves garlic, quartered

2 long green chillies, chopped coarsely

2 tablespoons lime juice

2 tablespoons peanut oil

1 tablespoon grated palm sugar

1 tablespoon fish sauce

1 Bring the water to a boil in medium saucepan; poach chicken, lemon grass, star anise and ginger, covered, about 10 minutes or until chicken is cooked through. Cool chicken in liquid 10 minutes. Strain and reserve cooking liquid; discard lemon grass, star anise and ginger. Slice chicken thinly.

2 Meanwhile, make nam jim dressing.

3 Heat oil in same cleaned saucepan; cook onion, stirring, until soft. Add rice; cook, stirring, 1 minute. Add reserved cooking liquid; bring to a boil. Reduce heat; simmer, uncovered, about 15 minutes or until rice is just tender. Drain; cool 10 minutes.

4 Meanwhile, boil, steam or microwave snow peas until just tender; drain. Rinse under cold water; drain.

5 Place chicken, rice and snow peas in large bowl with capsicum, mizuna, coriander and dressing; toss gently to combine.

NAM JIM DRESSING Blend or process ingredients until smooth.

PER SERVING 17.6g fat; 2173kJ (519 cal)

TIP You can use a barbecued chicken for this recipe; however, you will have to cook the rice in a mixture of water and prepared chicken stock instead of the cooking liquid.

MEAT

94

butter chicken with onion pilaf

preparation time 30 minutes (plus marinating time) **cooking time** 1 hour 45 minutes **serves** 4

1 cup (150g) raw cashews

2 teaspoons garam masala

2 teaspoons ground coriander

¾ teaspoon chilli powder

3 cloves garlic, chopped coarsely

2 teaspoons grated fresh ginger

2 tablespoons white vinegar

⅓ cup (80g) tomato paste

½ cup (140g) yogurt

1kg chicken thigh fillets, halved

80g butter

1 large brown onion (200g), chopped finely

1 cinnamon stick

4 cardamom pods, bruised

1 teaspoon paprika

400g canned tomato puree

¾ cup (180ml) chicken stock

1 cup (250ml) cream

ONION PILAF

40g butter

3 large brown onions (600g), chopped finely

1 tablespoon cumin seeds

3 cups (600g) basmati rice

6 cups (1.5 litres) chicken stock

1 Stir nuts, garam masala, coriander and chilli in heated small frying pan until nuts are browned lightly.

2 Blend or process nut mixture with garlic, ginger, vinegar, paste and half of the yogurt until just smooth. Transfer mixture to large bowl; combine nut mixture, remaining yogurt and chicken. Cover; refrigerate 3 hours or until required. (Can be made a day ahead to this stage and refrigerated, covered.)

3 Melt butter in large saucepan; cook onion, cinnamon and cardamom, stirring, until onion is browned. Add chicken mixture; cook 10 minutes.

4 Add paprika, puree and stock; bring to a boil. Reduce heat; simmer, uncovered, 45 minutes, stirring occasionally. (Can be made a day ahead to this stage and refrigerated, covered.)

5 Remove and discard cinnamon and cardamom. Add cream; simmer 5 minutes. Serve with onion pilaf.

ONION PILAF Melt butter in medium saucepan; cook onion and seeds, stirring, until onion is browned lightly. Add rice; cook, stirring, 1 minute. Stir in stock; bring to a boil. Reduce heat; simmer, covered tightly, about 25 minutes or until rice is just tender and liquid is absorbed. Remove from heat; fluff rice with fork. Stand, covered, 5 minutes.

PER SERVING *82.9g fat; 7297kJ (1744 cal)*

nasi goreng

preparation time 15 minutes cooking time 20 minutes serves 6

10g butter

2 eggs

1 tablespoon peanut oil

1 clove garlic, crushed

1 fresh red thai chilli, chopped finely

4 green onions, chopped finely

150g chicken thigh fillets, chopped finely

150g button mushrooms, sliced thinly

150g chinese barbecued pork, sliced thinly

1 small carrot (70g), sliced thinly

16 cooked shelled medium prawns

4 cups (600g) cooked jasmine rice

6 spinach leaves, shredded finely

1 tablespoon soy sauce

1 tablespoon tomato sauce

1 teaspoon hot paprika

1 Heat butter in heated large wok or frying pan; cook eggs, on one side only, until just set. Remove from wok.

2 Heat oil in wok; cook garlic, chilli and onion, stirring, until onion is just tender. Add chicken; cook, stirring, until chicken is tender.

3 Add mushrooms, pork, carrot, prawns, rice and spinach; cook, stirring, until combined and hot. Stir in sauces and paprika. Serve topped with eggs.
PER SERVING *12.5g fat; 1494kJ (357 cal)*

TIP Recipe can be made a day ahead and refrigerated, covered.

seasoned tofu pouches

preparation time 15 minutes **cooking time** 15 minutes **makes** 8

Ready-made seasoned bean-curd skins and seasoned gourd (seasoned kampyo) strips are available from Asian specialist grocery stores.

8 seasoned fried bean curd pouches (sweetened abura-age)

1 teaspoon toasted black sesame seeds

1 lebanese cucumber (130g),
halved, seeded, diced finely

1½ cups prepared sushi rice (see page 70)

medium bowl filled with cold water,
with 1 tablespoon rice vinegar added

8 strips seasoned gourd (seasoned kampyo)

1 teaspoon red pickled ginger (beni-shoga)

1 Carefully cut open pouches on one side, gently pushing fingers into each corner to form pouch.
2 Reserve a few of the seeds for garnish; fold remaining seeds and cucumber through rice.
3 Dip fingers of right hand in bowl of vinegared water, shake off excess. Pick up about an eighth of the rice with right hand; gently and loosely fit it into one pouch, being careful not to overfill or tear pouch and to push rice into pouch's corners.
4 Fold one side of pouch down over rice; fold the other side over the first and turn the pouch over so the join is underneath.
5 Tie a strip of gourd around pouch with a loose knot on top; garnish with a little red pickled ginger and reserved sesame seeds. Repeat with remaining ingredients.
PER PIECE *2.8g fat; 389kJ (93 cal)*

VEGETARIAN

brown rice, chickpea and pepita salad with kumara potato patties

preparation time 20 minutes cooking time 35 minutes serves 4

Pepitas, dried roasted pumpkin seeds, are popular both as a cooking ingredient or eaten on their own as a snack. They're easily found in most health food stores and supermarkets.

1½ cups (300g) brown rice

1 large kumara (500g), chopped coarsely

4 small potatoes (480g), chopped coarsely

2 tablespoons plain flour

2 tablespoons sour cream

2 tablespoons finely chopped fresh chives

¼ cup (35g) plain flour, extra

2 tablespoons vegetable oil

300g canned chickpeas, rinsed, drained

⅓ cup (55g) pepitas

⅓ cup (55g) raisins

3 trimmed celery stalks (300g), sliced thinly

2 tablespoons finely chopped fresh flat-leaf parsley

¼ cup finely chopped fresh mint

1 tablespoon finely grated lemon rind

1 medium red onion (170g), sliced thinly

3 small tomatoes (270g), chopped finely

TAHINI DRESSING

2 tablespoons tahini

½ cup (125ml) lemon juice

¼ cup (60ml) olive oil

1 Cook rice in large saucepan of boiling water, uncovered, until rice is tender; drain. Rinse under cold water; drain.

2 Meanwhile, boil, steam or microwave kumara and potato, separately, until tender; drain. Mash combined kumara and potato in large bowl; cool 10 minutes.

3 Make tahini dressing.

4 Stir flour, sour cream and chives into mashed kumara mixture. Using hands, shape mixture into eight patties; coat patties in extra flour. Heat oil in large heavy-base frying pan; cook patties, four at a time, until browned lightly both sides and heated through. Cover to keep warm.

5 Place rice in large bowl with dressing and remaining ingredients; toss gently to combine. Serve rice salad with patties.

TAHINI DRESSING Combine ingredients in screw-top jar; shake well.

PER SERVING *43.3g fat; 4046kJ (967 cal)*

tofu cakes with sweet chilli dipping sauce

preparation time 15 minutes (plus standing time) **cooking time** 15 minutes **makes** 20 cakes

You need to cook about ⅓ cup basmati rice for this recipe.

300g fresh firm tofu

1 cup (150g) cooked basmati rice

3 teaspoons red curry paste

2 green onions, chopped finely

1 tablespoon coarsely chopped fresh coriander

1 egg, beaten lightly

SWEET CHILLI DIPPING SAUCE

¼ cup (60ml) white vinegar

½ cup (110g) caster sugar

½ teaspoon salt

¾ cup (180ml) water

½ small red onion (50g), chopped finely

½ small carrot (35g), chopped finely

½ small lebanese cucumber (65g), seeded, chopped finely

2 tablespoons coarsely chopped fresh coriander

⅓ cup (80ml) sweet chilli sauce

1 Press tofu between two chopping boards or trays, place weight on top; elevate boards slightly to allow tofu liquid to drain away. Stand 20 minutes; chop coarsely. Blend or process tofu until smooth.

2 Preheat oven to 200°C/180°C fan-forced; line oven tray with baking paper.

3 Combine tofu in medium bowl with rice, paste, onion, coriander and egg.

4 Shape level tablespoons of the tofu mixture into rounds; place on oven tray. Bake, uncovered, in oven about 10 minutes or until lightly browned and heated through. Serve tofu cakes with sweet chilli dipping sauce.
SWEET CHILLI DIPPING SAUCE Place vinegar, sugar, salt and the water in small saucepan; bring to a boil. Boil, stirring, about 2 minutes or until sugar dissolves. Pour vinegar mixture over remaining ingredients in medium heatproof bowl; stir to combine.
PER CAKE *1.7g fat; 326kJ (78 cal)*

VEGETARIAN

104

citrus rice pudding

preparation time 15 minutes (plus standing time) **cooking time** 1 hour 10 minutes **serves** 8

2 cups (500ml) no-fat milk

1 vanilla bean, halved lengthways

1 teaspoon finely grated lemon rind

1 teaspoon finely grated lime rind

2 teaspoons finely grated orange rind

2 eggs

1 egg white

½ cup (110g) caster sugar

1½ cups (225g) cooked long-grain white rice

½ cup (125ml) low-fat cream

1   Preheat oven to 160°C/140°C fan-forced. Grease shallow oval 1.5-litre (6-cup) ovenproof dish.

2   Combine milk, vanilla bean and rinds in medium saucepan; bring to a boil. Remove from heat; stand, covered, 5 minutes.

3   Meanwhile, whisk eggs, egg white and sugar in medium bowl. Gradually whisk hot milk mixture into egg mixture; discard vanilla bean.

4   Spread rice into prepared dish; pour egg mixture carefully over rice. Place dish in large baking dish; add enough boiling water to baking dish to come halfway up side of pudding dish.

5   Bake, uncovered, in oven about 1 hour or until set. Serve warm with cream.
PER SERVING *4.8g fat; 1094kJ (261 cal)*

DESSERTS

baked rice custard

preparation time 10 minutes cooking time 1 hour 5 minutes serves 4

3 eggs

⅓ cup (75g) caster sugar

1 teaspoon vanilla extract

2½ cups (625ml) milk

½ cup cooked rice

¼ cup (40g) sultanas

½ teaspoon ground nutmeg or cinnamon

1　Preheat oven to 180°C/160°C fan-forced.

2　Whisk eggs, sugar, extract and milk together in medium bowl; add rice and sultanas.

3　Pour mixture into 1 litre (4-cup) ovenproof dish; place dish in baking dish. Add enough boiling water to come halfway up sides of dish.

4　Bake in oven 35 minutes. Slip fork under skin of custard; stir to distribute rice through custard evenly. Bake further 15 minutes; stir again using fork.

5　Sprinkle custard with nutmeg or cinnamon; cook further 15 minutes or until just set. Serve with raspberries, if desired.

PER SERVING *10.2g fat; 1236kJ (295 cal)*

creamed rice with fruit compote

preparation time 15 minutes cooking time 55 minutes serves 8

5 cups (1.25 litres) milk

½ cup (110g) white sugar

2 teaspoons rum essence

1 tablespoon vanilla extract

2 cups (400g) short-grain white rice

½ cup (60g) flaked almonds, toasted

FRUIT COMPOTE

415g canned apricot halves

½ cup (125ml) water

⅓ cup (80ml) orange juice

¼ cup (60ml) lemon juice

½ cup (110g) white sugar

⅔ cup (110g) seeded prunes

⅓ cup (50g) dried currants

2 cinnamon sticks

1 teaspoon finely grated lemon rind

1 Combine milk, sugar, essence and extract in medium pan; bring to boil, stirring. Gradually stir in rice; cover pan tightly, simmer over very low heat, stirring occasionally, about 25 minutes or until most of the liquid is absorbed. (Best made just before serving.)

2 Serve rice, sprinkled with almonds, with fruit compote.
FRUIT COMPOTE Drain apricot halves over medium pan. Add the water, juices and sugar; stir over heat, without boiling, until sugar dissolves. Simmer, uncovered, without stirring, for about 5 minutes or until syrup thickens slightly. Add prunes, currants, cinnamon sticks and rind to syrup; simmer, uncovered, stirring occasionally, about 10 minutes or until fruit is plump. Remove from heat, then stir in apricot halves.
PER SERVING *10.7g fat; 2077kJ (497 cal)*

creamed rice with stewed apples

preparation time 15 minutes cooking time 1 hour serves 4

½ cup (100g) short-grain rice

4 cups (1 litre) milk

½ cup (110g) white sugar

1 teaspoon vanilla extract

STEWED APPLES

2 medium apples (300g)

½ cup (125ml) water

1 tablespoon white sugar

1   Rinse rice in strainer under cold running water until water runs clear; drain well. Combine milk and sugar in medium heavy-base saucepan; bring to a boil. Add rice; reduce heat to lowest setting. Cover with tight-fitting lid. Rice must be cooked gently, just barely simmering, or it will burn onto base of pan.

2   Cook about 1 hour, stirring several times during cooking to make sure rice has not stuck to base of pan. Cook until almost all of the milk has been absorbed. Add essence; serve hot with stewed apples. Sprinkle with cinnamon, if desired.

STEWED APPLES Peel apples; cut into quarters. Remove core; slice apple. Bring the water and sugar to a boil in medium saucepan; add apple. Cover; return to a boil. Reduce heat; simmer, covered, about 5 minutes or until apple is just tender. Apple can be drained or served with the syrup.

PER SERVING *10g fat; 1670kJ (399 cal)*

BEETROOT also known as red beets; firm, round root vegetable. Can be grated or finely chopped; boiled or steamed then diced or sliced; or roasted then mashed.

BROAD BEANS also known as fava, windsor and horse beans; available dried, fresh, canned and frozen. Fresh and frozen forms should be peeled twice (discarding both the outer long green pod and the beige-green tough inner shell) then eaten in salads, tossed through pasta or pureed.

BUK CHOY also known as bok choy, pak choi, Chinese white cabbage or Chinese chard; has a fresh, mild mustard taste. Use both stems and leaves, stir-fried or braised. Baby buk choy, also known as pak kat farang or shanghai bok choy, is much smaller and more tender than buk choy. Its mildly acrid, distinctively appealing taste has made it one of the most commonly used Asian greens.

CAPSICUM also known as pepper or bell pepper. Native to central and South America; found in red, green, yellow, orange or purplish-black varieties. Seeds and membranes should be discarded before use.

CHEESE
parmesan also known as parmigiano, parmesan is a hard, grainy cow-milk cheese. Parmesan is grated or flaked and used for pasta, salads and soups; it is also eaten on its own with fruit.
pecorino the generic name for cheeses made from sheep milk. If you can't find it, use parmesan.

CHICKPEAS also called garbanzos, hummus or channa; an irregularly round, sandy-coloured legume used extensively in Mediterranean, Indian and Hispanic cooking. Firm texture even after cooking, a floury mouth-feel and robust nutty flavour; available canned or dried (the latter need several hours reconstituting in cold water before being used).

CORIANDER also known as cilantro, pak chee or chinese parsley; bright-green-leafed herb having both pungent aroma and taste. Both the stems and roots of coriander are used in Thai cooking: wash well before chopping or adding to food.

CURRY PASTES make your own or purchase ready-made pastes found in supermarkets.
balti a medium-hot, aromatic paste with coriander, fenugreek and mint, which gives it its distinctive mild "green" flavour.
red probably the most popular Thai curry paste; a hot blend of different flavours that complements the richness of pork, duck and seafood. Also works well stirred into marinades and sauces.

DAIKON also known as white radish; an everyday fixture at the Japanese table, this long, white horseradish has a wonderful, sweet flavour. After peeling, eat it raw in salads or shredded as a garnish; also great when sliced or cubed and cooked in stir-fries and casseroles. The flesh is white but the skin can be white or black; buy those that are firm and unwrinkled from Asian food shops.

DASHI the basic fish and seaweed stock that accounts for the distinctive flavour of many Japanese dishes, such as soups and various casserole dishes. Made from dried bonito (a type of tuna) flakes and kombu (kelp); instant dashi (dashi-no-moto) is available in powder, granules and liquid concentrate from Asian food shops.

EGGPLANT also known as aubergine; often thought of as a vegetable but actually a fruit and belongs to the same family as the tomato, chilli and potato. Ranging in size from tiny to very large and in colour from pale green to deep purple. Can be purchased char-grilled, packed in oil, in jars.
finger also known as baby or Japanese eggplant; very small and slender so can be used without disgorging.

FISH SAUCE called naam pla on the label if Thai-made, nuoc naam if Vietnamese; the two are almost identical. Made from pulverised salted fermented fish (most often anchovies); has a pungent smell and strong taste. Available in varying degrees of intensity, so use according to your taste.

GARAM MASALA literally meaning blended spices in its northern Indian place of origin; based on varying proportions of cardamom, cinnamon, cloves, coriander, fennel and cumin, roasted and ground together.

GHEE clarified butter; with the milk solids removed, this fat has a high smoking point so can be heated to a high temperature without burning. Used as a cooking medium in most Indian recipes.

GREEN ONION also known as scallion or (incorrectly) shallot; an immature onion picked before the bulb has formed, having a long, bright-green edible stalk.

KUMARA the polynesian name of an orange-fleshed sweet potato often confused with yam; good baked, boiled, mashed or fried similarly to other potatoes.

LEBANESE CUCUMBER short, slender and thin-skinned. Probably the most popular variety because of its tender, edible skin, tiny, yielding seeds, and sweet, fresh and flavoursome taste.

LEEKS a member of the onion family, the leek resembles a green onion but is much larger and more subtle in flavour. Tender baby or pencil leeks can be eaten whole with minimal cooking but adult leeks are usually trimmed then chopped or sliced and cooked as an ingredient in stews and soups.

MIRIN a Japanese champagne-coloured cooking wine, made of glutinous rice and alcohol. It is used expressly for cooking and should not be confused with sake.
A seasoned sweet mirin, manjo mirin, made of water, rice, corn syrup and alcohol, is used in various Japanese dipping sauces.

MIZUNA Japanese in origin; frizzy green salad leaves with a delicate mustard flavour.

MUSHROOMS
button small, cultivated white mushrooms with a mild flavour. When a recipe in this book calls for an unspecified type of mushroom, use button.
dried shiitake also known as donko or dried Chinese mushrooms; have a unique meaty flavour. Sold dried; rehydrate before use.
oyster also known as abalone; grey-white mushrooms shaped like a fan. Smooth textured with a subtle, oyster-like flavour.
shiitake fresh, are also known as Chinese black, forest or golden oak mushrooms. Although cultivated, they have the earthiness and taste of wild mushrooms.

GLOSSARY

swiss brown also known as roman or cremini. Light to dark brown mushrooms with full-bodied flavour; suited for use in casseroles or being stuffed and baked.

NORI a type of dried seaweed used in Japanese cooking as a flavouring, garnish or for sushi. Sold in thin sheets, plain or toasted (yaki-nori).

OIL

peanut pressed from ground peanuts; the most commonly used oil in Asian cooking because of its high smoke point (capacity to handle high heat without burning).

sesame made from roasted, crushed, white sesame seeds; a flavouring rather than a cooking medium.

PANCETTA an Italian unsmoked bacon, pork belly cured in salt and spices then rolled into a sausage shape and dried for several weeks. Used, sliced or chopped, as an ingredient rather than eaten on its own; can also be used to add taste and moisture to tough or dry cuts of meat. Used in pasta sauces and meat dishes.

PARSLEY an extremely versatile herb with a fresh, slightly earthy flavour. There are about 30 varieties of curly parsley; the flat-leaf variety (also known as continental or Italian parsley) is stronger in flavour and darker in colour.

PATTY-PAN SQUASH also known as crookneck or custard marrow pumpkins; a round, slightly flat summer squash being yellow to pale green in colour and having a scalloped edge. Harvested young, it has firm white flesh and a distinct flavour.

PICKLED GINGER pink or red coloured; available, packaged, from Asian food shops. Pickled paper-thin shavings of ginger in a mixture of vinegar, sugar and natural colouring; most used in Japanese cooking.

PROSCIUTTO a kind of unsmoked Italian ham; salted, air-cured and aged, it is usually eaten uncooked. There are many styles of prosciutto available, one of the best being Parma ham, from Italy's Emilia Romagna region, which is traditionally lightly salted, dried then eaten raw.

RICE

arborio small, round-grain rice well-suited to absorb a large amount of liquid; the high level of starch makes it especially suitable for risottos, giving the dish its classic creaminess.

basmati a white, fragrant long-grained rice; the grains fluff up beautifully when cooked. It should be washed several times before being cooked.

jasmine or Thai jasmine, is a long-grained white rice recognised around the world as having a perfumed aromatic quality; moist in texture, it clings together after cooking. Sometimes substituted for basmati rice.

long-grain elongated grains that remain separate when cooked; this is the most popular steaming rice in Asia.

short-grain fat, almost round grain with a high starch content; tends to clump together when cooked.

white is hulled and polished rice, can be short- or long-grained.

wild not a true member of the rice family but a very dark brown seed of a North American aquatic grass having a distinctively nutty flavour and crunchy, resilient texture. Sold on its own or in a blend with basmati or long-grain white rice.

ROCKET also known as arugula, rugula and rucola; peppery green leaf eaten raw in salads or used in cooking. Baby rocket leaves are smaller and less peppery.

SAFFRON stigma of a member of the crocus family, available ground or in strands; imparts a yellow-orange colour to food once infused. The quality can vary greatly; the best is the most expensive spice in the world.

SEAFOOD

crab meat flesh of fresh crabs, frozen flesh is also available. Use canned if either is unavailable.

mussels should be bought from a fish market where there is reliably fresh fish; they must be tightly closed when bought, indicating they are alive. Before cooking, scrub the shells with a strong brush and remove the beards; discard any shells that do not open after cooking. Varieties include black and green-lip.

prawns also known as shrimp. Varieties include, school, king, royal red, Sydney harbour, tiger. Can be bought uncooked (green) or cooked, with or without shells.

ocean trout a farmed fish with pink, soft flesh. It is from the same family as the atlantic salmon; one can be substituted for the other.

STAR ANISE a dried star-shaped pod whose seeds have an astringent aniseed flavour; commonly used to flavour stocks and marinades.

SUGAR we use coarse, granulated table sugar, also known as crystal sugar, unless otherwise specified.

brown an extremely soft, fine granulated sugar retaining molasses for its characteristic colour and flavour.

caster also known as superfine or finely granulated table sugar. The fine crystals dissolve easily so it is perfect for cakes, meringues and desserts.

palm also known as nam tan pip, jaggery, jawa or gula melaka; made from the sap of the sugar palm tree. Light brown to black in colour and usually sold in rock-hard cakes; substitute with brown sugar if unavailable.

SUGAR SNAP PEAS also known as honey snap peas; fresh small pea which can be eaten whole, pod and all.

TAHINI sesame seed paste available from Middle Eastern food stores; most often used in hummus and baba ghanoush.

TERIYAKI either home-made or commercially bottled, this Japanese sauce, made from soy sauce, mirin, sugar, ginger and other spices, imparts a distinctive glaze when brushed over grilled meat or poultry.

THAI CHILLI also known as "scuds"; tiny, very hot and bright red in colour.

THYME a member of the mint family; there are many types of this herb but two that we use most. The "household" variety, simply called thyme in most shops, is French thyme; it has tiny grey-green leaves that give off a pungent minty, light-lemon aroma. Dried thyme comes in both leaf and powdered form. Lemon thyme's scent is due to the high level of citral in its leaves, an oil also found in lemon, orange, verbena and lemon grass. The citrus scent is enhanced by crushing the leaves in your hands before using the herb.

TOFU also known as soybean curd or bean curd; an off-white, custard-like product made from the "milk" of crushed soybeans. Comes fresh as soft or firm, and processed as fried or pressed dried sheets. Fresh tofu can be refrigerated in water (changed daily) for up to four days.

WASABI an Asian horseradish used to make the pungent, green-coloured sauce traditionally served with Japanese raw fish dishes; sold in powdered or paste form.

ZUCCHINI also known as courgette; small, pale- or dark-green, yellow or white vegetable belonging to the squash family. Harvested when young, its edible flowers can be stuffed with a mild cheese or other similarly delicate ingredients then deep-fried or oven-baked to make a delicious appetiser. Good cored and stuffed with various meat or rice fillings; in Italian vegetable dishes and pasta sauces; and as one of the vegetables that make ratatouille.

MEASURES

One Australian metric measuring cup holds approximately 250ml; one Australian metric tablespoon holds 20ml; one Australian metric teaspoon holds 5ml.

The difference between one country's measuring cups and another's is within a two- or three-teaspoon variance, and will not affect your cooking results. North America, New Zealand and the United Kingdom use a 15ml tablespoon.

All cup and spoon measurements are level. The most accurate way of measuring dry ingredients is to weigh them. When measuring liquids, use a clear glass or plastic jug with the metric markings.

We use large eggs with an average weight of 60g.

DRY MEASURES

METRIC	IMPERIAL
15g	½oz
30g	1oz
60g	2oz
90g	3oz
125g	4oz (¼lb)
155g	5oz
185g	6oz
220g	7oz
250g	8oz (½lb)
280g	9oz
315g	10oz
345g	11oz
375g	12oz (¾lb)
410g	13oz
440g	14oz
470g	15oz
500g	16oz (1lb)
750g	24oz (1½lb)
1kg	32oz (2lb)

LIQUID MEASURES

METRIC	IMPERIAL
30ml	1 fluid oz
60ml	2 fluid oz
100ml	3 fluid oz
125ml	4 fluid oz
150ml	5 fluid oz (¼ pint/1 gill)
190ml	6 fluid oz
250ml	8 fluid oz
300ml	10 fluid oz (½ pint)
500ml	16 fluid oz
600ml	20 fluid oz (1 pint)
1000ml (1 litre)	1¾ pints

LENGTH MEASURES

METRIC	IMPERIAL
3mm	⅛in
6mm	¼in
1cm	½in
2cm	¾in
2.5cm	1in
5cm	2in
6cm	2½in
8cm	3in
10cm	4in
13cm	5in
15cm	6in
18cm	7in
20cm	8in
23cm	9in
25cm	10in
28cm	11in
30cm	12in (1ft)

OVEN TEMPERATURES

These oven temperatures are only a guide for conventional ovens. For fan-forced ovens, check the manufacturer's manual.

	°C (CELSIUS)	°F (FAHRENHEIT)	GAS MARK
Very slow	120	250	½
Slow	150	275-300	1-2
Moderately slow	160	325	3
Moderate	180	350-375	4-5
Moderately hot	200	400	6
Hot	220	425-450	7-8
Very hot	240	475	9

CONVERSION CHART

INDEX

ARE YOU MISSING SOME OF THE WORLD'S FAVOURITE COOKBOOKS?

The Australian Women's Weekly Cookbooks are available from bookshops, cookshops, supermarkets and other stores all over the world. You can also buy direct from the publisher, using the order form below.

ACP Magazines Ltd Privacy Notice
This book may contain offers, competitions or surveys that require you to provide information about yourself if you choose to enter or take part in any such Reader Offer. If you provide information about yourself to ACP Magazines Ltd, the company will use this information to provide you with the products or services you have requested, and may supply your information to contractors that help ACP to do this. ACP will also use your information to inform you of other ACP publications, products, services and events. ACP will also give your information to organisations that are providing special prizes or offers, and that are clearly associated with the Reader Offer. Unless you tell us not to, we may give your information to other organisations that use it to inform you about other products, services and events or who may give it to other organisations that may use it for this purpose. If you would like to gain access to the information ACP holds about you, please contact ACP's Privacy Officer at ACP Magazines Ltd, 54-58 Park Street, Sydney, NSW 2000, Australia.

☐ **Privacy Notice** Please do not provide information about me to any organisation not associated with this offer.

To order: Mail or fax – photocopy or complete the order form above, and send your credit card details or cheque payable to: Australian Consolidated Press (UK), ACP Books, 10 Scirocco Close, Moulton Park Office Village, Northampton NN3 6AP
phone (+44) (0)1604 642200
fax (+44) (0)1604 642300
email books@acpuk.com
or order online at www.acpuk.com
Non-UK residents: We accept the credit cards listed on the coupon, or cheques, drafts or International Money Orders payable in sterling and drawn on a UK bank. Credit card charges are at the exchange rate current at the time of payment.
Postage and packing UK: Add £1.00 per order plus £1.75 per book.
Postage and packing overseas: Add £2.00 per order plus £3.50 per book.
All pricing current at time of going to press and subject to change/availability.
Offer ends 31.12.2008

TITLE	RRP	QTY	TITLE	RRP	QTY
100 Fast Fillets	£6.99		Indian Cooking Class	£6.99	
After Work Fast	£6.99		Japanese Cooking Class	£6.99	
Beginners Cooking Class	£6.99		Just For One	£6.99	
Beginners Thai	£6.99		Just For Two	£6.99	
Best Food Desserts	£6.99		Kids' Birthday Cakes	£6.99	
Best Food Fast	£6.99		Kids Cooking	£6.99	
Breads & Muffins	£6.99		Kids' Cooking Step-by-Step	£6.99	
Cafe Classics	£6.99		Low-carb, Low-fat	£6.99	
Cakes Bakes & Desserts	£6.99		Low-fat Feasts	£6.99	
Cakes Biscuits & Slices	£6.99		Low-fat Food for Life	£6.99	
Cakes Cooking Class	£6.99		Low-fat Meals in Minutes	£6.99	
Caribbean Cooking	£6.99		Main Course Salads	£6.99	
Casseroles	£6.99		Mexican	£6.99	
Casseroles & Slow-Cooked Classics	£6.99		Middle Eastern Cooking Class	£6.99	
Cheap Eats	£6.99		Mince in Minutes	£6.99	
Cheesecakes: baked and chilled	£6.99		Moroccan & the Foods of North Africa	£6.99	
Chicken	£6.99		Muffins, Scones & Breads	£6.99	
Chicken Meals in Minutes	£6.99		New Casseroles	£6.99	
Chinese & the foods of Thailand, Vietnam, Malaysia & Japan	£6.99		New Curries	£6.99	
			New Finger Food	£6.99	
Chinese Cooking Class	£6.99		New French Food	£6.99	
Christmas Cooking	£6.99		New Salads	£6.99	
Chocolate	£6.99		Party Food and Drink	£6.99	
Chocs & Treats	£6.99		Pasta Meals in Minutes	£6.99	
Cocktails	£6.99		Potatoes	£6.99	
Cookies & Biscuits	£6.99		Rice & Risotto	£6.99	
Cupcakes & Fairycakes	£6.99		Salads: Simple, Fast & Fresh	£6.99	
Detox	£6.99		Sauces Salsas & Dressings	£6.99	
Dinner Lamb	£6.99		Sensational Stir-Fries	£6.99	
Dinner Seafood	£6.99		Simple Healthy Meals	£6.99	
Easy Curry	£6.99		Soup	£6.99	
Easy Midweek Meals	£6.99		Stir-fry	£6.99	
Easy Spanish-Style	£6.99		Superfoods for Exam Success	£6.99	
Essential Soup	£6.99		Sweet Old-Fashioned Favourites	£6.99	
Food for Fit and Healthy Kids	£6.99		Tapas Mezze Antipasto & other bites	£6.99	
Foods of the Mediterranean	£6.99		Thai Cooking Class	£6.99	
Foods That Fight Back	£6.99		Traditional Italian	£6.99	
Fresh Food Fast	£6.99		Vegetarian Meals in Minutes	£6.99	
Fresh Food for Babies & Toddlers	£6.99		Vegie Food	£6.99	
Good Food for Babies & Toddlers	£6.99		Wicked Sweet Indulgences	£6.99	
Greek Cooking Class	£6.99		Wok Meals in Minutes	£6.99	
Grills	£6.99				
Healthy Heart Cookbook	£6.99		TOTAL COST:	£	

Mr/Mrs/Ms _____

Address _____

_____ Postcode _____

Day time phone _____ Email* (optional) _____

I enclose my cheque/money order for £ _____

or please charge £ _____

to my: ☐ Access ☐ Mastercard ☐ Visa ☐ Diners Club

Card number [ ][ ][ ][ ][ ][ ][ ][ ][ ][ ][ ][ ][ ][ ][ ][ ]

Expiry date _____ 3 digit security code *(found on reverse of card)* _____

Cardholder's name _____ Signature _____

* By including your email address, you consent to receipt of any email regarding this magazine, and other emails which inform you of ACP's other publications, products, services and events, and to promote third party goods and services you may be interested in.

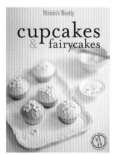
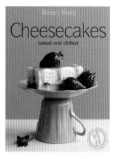

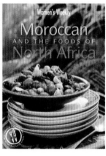

You'll find these books and more available on sale at bookshops, cookshops, selected supermarkets or direct from the publisher (see order form page 119).

TEST KITCHEN
Food director Pamela Clark
Test Kitchen manager Kellie-Marie Thomas
Nutritional information Belinda Farlow

ACP BOOKS
General manager Christine Whiston
Editorial director Susan Tomnay
Creative director Hieu Chi Nguyen
Designer Hannah Blackmore
Director of sales Brian Cearnes
Marketing manager Bridget Cody
Business analyst Ashley Davies
Operations manager David Scotto
International rights enquires Laura Bamford
lbamford@acpuk.com

ACP Books are published by ACP Magazines
a division of PBL Media Pty Limited
Group publisher, Women's lifestyle
Pat Ingram
Director of sales, Women's lifestyle
Lynette Phillips
Commercial manager, Women's lifestyle
Seymour Cohen
Marketing director, Women's lifestyle
Matthew Dominello
Public relations manager, Women's lifestyle
Hannah Deveraux
Creative director, Events, Women's lifestyle
Luke Bonnano
Research Director, Women's lifestyle
Justin Stone
ACP Magazines, Chief Executive officer
Scott Lorson
PBL Media, Chief Executive officer
Ian Law

Produced by ACP Books, Sydney.
Published by ACP Books, a division of
ACP Magazines Ltd, 54 Park St, Sydney;
GPO Box 4088, Sydney, NSW 2001.
phone (02) 9282 8618 fax (02) 9267 9438.
acpbooks@acpmagazines.com.au
www.acpbooks.com.au
Printed by Dai Nippon in Korea.

Australia Distributed by Network Services,
phone +61 2 9282 8777 fax +61 2 9264 3278
networkweb@networkservicescompany.com.au
United Kingdom Distributed by Australian
Consolidated Press (UK),
phone (01604) 642 200 fax (01604) 642 300
books@acpuk.com
New Zealand Distributed by Netlink
Distribution Company,
phone (9) 366 9966 ask@ndc.co.nz
South Africa Distributed by PSD Promotions,
phone (27 11) 392 6065/6/7
fax (27 11) 392 6079/80
orders@psdprom.co.za

Rice and risotto.
Includes index.
ISBN 978 1 86396 717 4 (pbk)
1. Cookery (Rice). 2. Risotto.
I Clark, Pamela. II Title: Australian Women's Weekly
641.6318
© ACP Magazines Ltd 2007
ABN 18 053 273 546
This publication is copyright. No part of it may be
reproduced or transmitted in any form without the
written permission of the publishers.
To order books,
phone 136 116 (within Australia).
Send recipe enquiries to:
recipeenquiries@acpmagazines.com.au